THE POWER TO KNOW®

SAS® 9.2 SQL Query Window
User's Guide

SAS® Documentation

The correct bibliographic citation for this manual is as follows: SAS Institute Inc. 2009. *SAS® 9.2 SQL Query Window User's Guide*. Cary, NC: SAS Institute Inc.

SAS® 9.2 SQL Query Window User's Guide

ISBN 978-1-59047-969-8

SAS Institute Inc., SAS Campus Drive, Cary, North Carolina 27513.

1st electronic book, February 2009
1st printing, March 2009

Contents

CHAPTER

1

An Overview of the SQL Query Window

Introduction

Structured Query Language (SQL) is a language that retrieves and updates data in relational tables and databases. SAS implements SQL through the SQL procedure.

The SQL Query Window is an interactive interface that enables you to build, save, and run queries (requests to retrieve data) without being familiar with SQL or with the SAS SQL procedure. The query that you build in the SQL Query Window is passed to the SQL procedure or to the REPORT procedure for processing when you run the query.

The SQL Query Window also provides you with the following capabilities:

- □ You can create PROC SQL tables (SAS data files) and views.
- □ If you have SAS/ACCESS software installed for your database management system (DBMS), then you can query DBMS data by using PROC SQL Pass-Through. Some SAS/ACCESS interfaces enable you to access data using a library engine. Library engine technology enables you to assign a libref to DBMS data and work with the data in the same way that you would with data in a SAS library. For more information, refer to the SAS/ACCESS documentation for your DBMS.
- □ If SAS/CONNECT software is licensed at your site, then you can use the SQL Query Window to access data that is stored on remote hosts.
- □ You can use PROC REPORT to design a report from your query output without exiting the SQL Query Window.

After exiting the SQL Query Window, you can use your query output with other SAS procedures and SAS/ASSIST software to perform various other functions such as analyzing your data or producing graphics.

For more information about the SQL and REPORT procedures, refer to the *Base SAS Procedures Guide*.

Invoking the SQL Query Window

You can invoke the SQL Query Window in one of the following ways:

- □ In the SAS command window or at the **Command ===>** prompt, issue the **QUERY** command.

  You can also specify these optional arguments:

profile=
: the name of a user-defined profile that you want to use for your SQL Query Window session. You can specify a profile by using the following syntax:

```
profile=libref.catalog.profile
```

access=
: the access mode (source of the data that you are going to use) for the SQL Query Window session.

active= *or* data=
: the name of the table (active SAS data set) that you want to use in your initial query.

  You can select more than one table by using the following syntax:

```
data='table1, table2'
```

  where *table1* and *table2* are the names of the tables that you want to use in your initial query.

  If you use this argument, then the SQL Query Window is invoked with the table or tables already selected, and you go directly to the SQL QUERY COLUMNS window.

include=
: the name of a stored query that you want to include in your SQL Query Window session. You can include a stored query by using the following syntax:

```
include=libref.catalog.query
```

  where *libref* is the library reference, *catalog* is the catalog in which the query is stored, and *query* is the query name.

If you use this argument, then the SQL Query Window is invoked with the query components already selected, and you go directly to the SQL QUERY COLUMNS window.

- From any SAS window, select**Tools ▶ Query**.
- If SAS/ASSIST software is installed at your site, then you can follow this selection path: **Tasks ▶ Data Management ▶ Query ▶ SQL Query**.
- From a SAS/AF application, the method that you use depends on whether the application has a frame or program screen.
  - If the application has a frame or program screen, then you can invoke it with this command:

    ```
    SUBMIT COMMAND CONTINUE;
       QUERY
    ENDF SUBMIT;
    ```

    Following the **QUERY** statement, you can specify any of the optional arguments that were described earlier for the command window or **Command ===>** prompt.
  - If the application has no frame or program screen, then you can invoke it with a **CALL EXECCMD** statement:

    ```
    CALL EXECCMD ('QUERY');
    ```

    Optional arguments can follow the word **QUERY** and must precede the closing quotation mark.

Query Window Menus

The SQL Query Window has **File**, **Tools**, **View**, and **Profile** items on the menu bar. Some items in a menu might appear dimmed, which means that they cannot be selected until you have performed some other action.

Note: The items that are described here are specific to the SQL Query Window. Other items that are on the menus are related to general SAS functionality. See the SAS System Help for more information about these items. △

File Menu

Save Query

This item displays a menu from which you can select these options:

Save as QUERY to include later
saves your query as a QUERY catalog entry. You can include the saved query during your current SQL Query Window session or during a later session. Other users who have access to the catalog in which the query is stored can also include the query in their sessions.

Save as SOURCE entry
saves your query as a SOURCE catalog entry. A query that is saved as a .SOURCE entry can be used in SAS/AF and SAS/EIS applications, and it can be included in the SAS Program Editor, but it cannot be included in the SQL Query Window.

`Save as External file`
saves your query as a PROC SQL statement in an external file.

For all of these ways to save a query, the query is stored on the local host even if you are connected to a remote session through SAS/CONNECT software.

List/Include Saved Queries

This item displays a list of the queries that you have previously saved in the Profile catalog with which the SQL Query Window was invoked. You can also display a list of queries that were saved in other catalogs. If the SQL Query Window was invoked without a profile, then the default Profile catalog is SASUSER.PROFILE.

Create Table from Query Results

This item enables you to create a PROC SQL table, which is a SAS data set, and to save the results of your query into it. If SAS/CONNECT software is licensed at your site and you select this item when you are connected to a remote session, then you can choose to download the results of your query into a local SAS data set, or create the table on the remote system.

Create View of Query

This item enables you to create a PROC SQL view that contains the SQL syntax of your query. The PROC SQL view can be read by any SAS procedure as if the view were a SAS data set. When you specify the view in a PROC or DATA step, the query is processed and returns current data from the queried table or tables to your report. If SAS/CONNECT software is licensed at your site and you select this item when you are connected to a remote session, then the view will be created on the remote system.

View Menu

Columns

This item enables you to

- select the columns that you want to include in your query
- set summary functions for columns
- build new computed columns to include in your query.

Where Conditions for Subset

This item enables you to use a WHERE expression to read a subset of the data in a table or tables by specifying the conditions that the selected data must meet.

Distinct

This item removes duplicate rows from your query output.

Order By

This item enables you to select columns or column expressions to specify the order by which you want the output sorted.

Group(s) for Summary Functions

This item enables you to specify groups of column values to which a function is to be applied.

Having Condition for Group

This item enables you to build or modify a HAVING expression. A HAVING expression specifies a condition (or conditions) for each group that is included in the query. You specify the group in a Group By clause. If no Group By clause is specified, then the rows in a table or a subset of the table are evaluated as one group.

Tables

This item enables you to select the table or tables from which you want to retrieve data. This is the first step in the query-building process. If you have already started building your query, then use the **Tables** item to

- select an additional table or tables for your query
- remove a table or tables from the current query
- select a table or tables for a new query.

Join Type

This item enables you to use inner joins or outer joins to join tables when you have selected two tables for the query.

Tools Menu

Run Query

This item displays a menu from which you can select these options:

Run Immediate
immediately submits the query to the SQL procedure for processing. The output appears in the Output window. If SAS/CONNECT software is licensed at your site and you select this item when you are connected to a remote session, then the query is submitted to the remote session for processing.

Design a Report
uses the REPORT procedure to design a report for your query output. Another menu appears with the following options:

> **Begin with default report**
> invokes PROC REPORT with the default settings for the query. You can then design a report within PROC REPORT.
>
> **Name a predefined report**
> lists any report definitions that have been stored in the catalog from which you invoked your SQL Query Window session or in other catalogs.
>
> **Use definition from last report**
> invokes PROC REPORT and uses the report definition that you designed when you selected **Design a Report** for your current query.

Show Query

This item displays the PROC SQL syntax for your query. You can choose this item at any time during the query-building process.

Preview Window

This item displays your query in a PREVIEW window. You can edit the query syntax in this window and save it to a file. Changes that you make in the PREVIEW window are not reflected in the current query in the SQL Query Window.

Switch Access Mode

This item enables you to specify whether you are going to query SAS data files (including SAS data sets and SAS data views) or tables from a database management system (DBMS). You can change the access mode at any time during an SQL Query Window session. Changing access modes resets the query and displays the tables that are available for that access mode.

Depending upon your operating environment and the SAS/ACCESS products that have been installed at your site, you can select one of the following access modes:

- SAS
- DB2
- ODBC
- ORACLE
- Sybase
- SQLDS
- RDB
- DB2/2
- INGRES
- INFORMIX
- DB2/6000.

Switch to New Profile

This item resets the query and enables you to change to a profile that was previously created and stored.

Reset

This item deletes your current query from the SQL Query Window and returns you to the Tables window to begin a new query.

Report Options

This item enables you to specify the beginning page number, title, and subtitles for the report.

Profile Menu

Set Preferences

This item enables you to create a profile entry.

Show Current Preferences

This item displays the preference settings that are in effect for your current SQL Query Window session.

Update Preferences

This item enables you to update the preference settings for any SQL Query Window profile.

Pop-Up Menu

If your system supports the use of a mouse, you can also display the most frequently used `Tools` and `View` items from the pop-up menu. To invoke the pop-up menu, click the rightmost mouse button anywhere in the SQL Query Window.

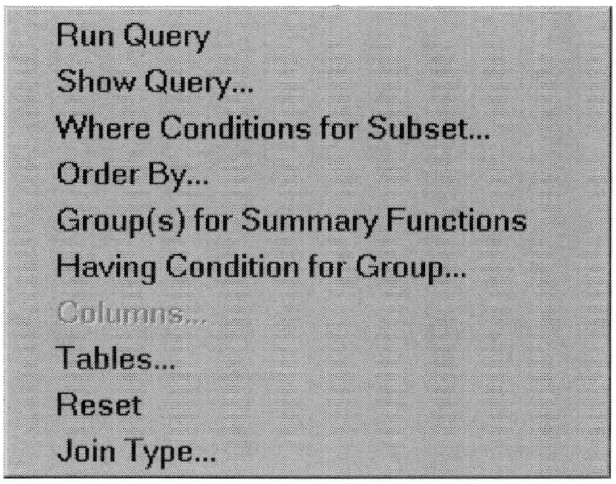

CHAPTER

2

Examples

Setting Up the Environment

To practice with the examples in this chapter, you will need to use the sample data library that is provided with the SQL Query Window.

Submit the following statement in the Program Editor to assign the SAMPLE libref to the sample library:

```
libname sample 'sample library';
```

Consult your on-site SAS support personnel for the location of the sample library. Some of the examples require that you save files to the sample library. If you do not have write access to the sample library, you can save the files to another library of your choice, such as the SASUSER library.

Invoking the Query Window

For these examples, invoke the SQL Query Window by selecting **Tools ▸ Query** or by entering **query** in the command window or at the **Command ===>** prompt.

The SQL QUERY TABLES window appears. By default, the SASUSER libref is selected and the tables from that libref appear in the Available Tables list.

Changing Your Profile

In order to include the tables that are in the sample library in the Available Tables list, you must set your SQL Query Window profile to include the tables in the SAMPLE library. Select **Profile ▸ Set Preferences**.

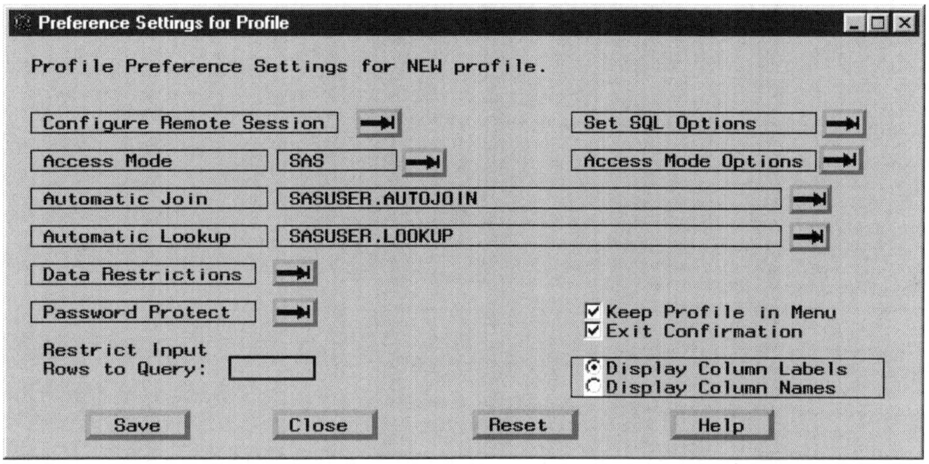

Select the right arrow next to Data Restrictions to display the Data Restrictions for Profile window.

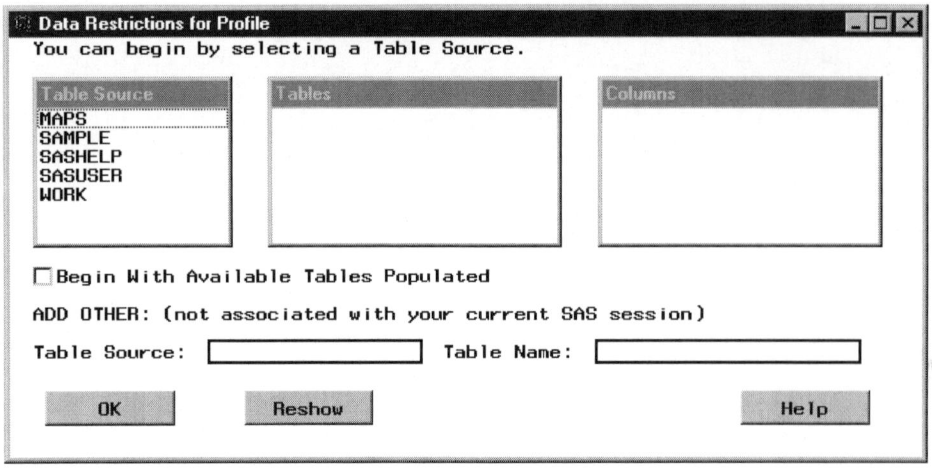

Select **SAMPLE** from the Table Source list. Select **Add entire Table Source to preferences** from the pop-up menu that appears.

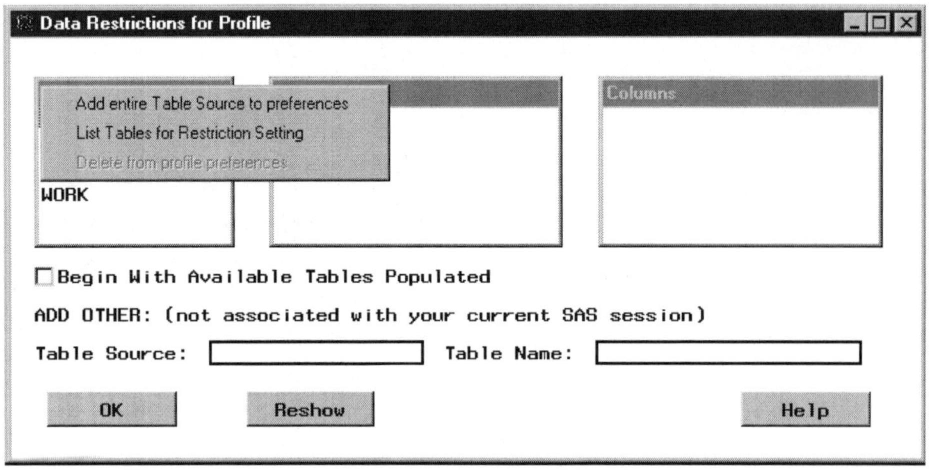

Select **WORK** from the Table Source list. Select **Add entire Table Source to preferences** from the pop-up menu.

Note: If you do not have write access to the SAMPLE library, then repeat the previous step for the SASUSER library. △

Select OK to return to the Preference Settings for Profile window.
Select Save to save your new profile setting.

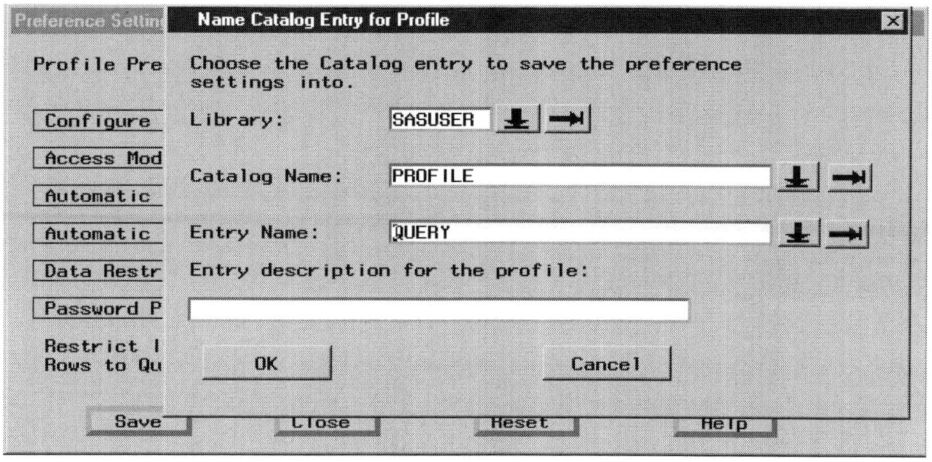

Type **SAMPLE** in the Entry Name field of the Name Catalog Entry for Profile window. Select [OK].

Select [Close] in the Preference Settings for Profile window.

From the SQL QUERY TABLES window, select **Tools ▶ Switch to New Profile**.

Select the right arrow next to the Profile Name field to display a list of profiles.

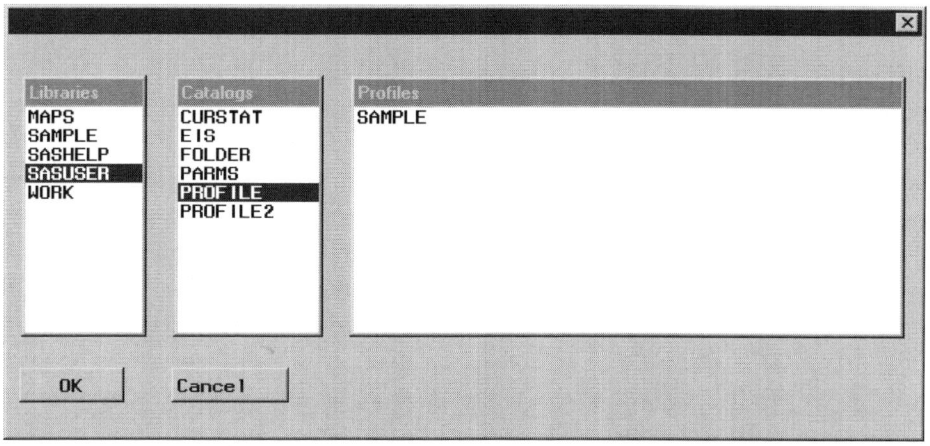

In the Preference Profiles in Catalog window, select **SASUSER** from the Libraries list. Next, select **PROFILE** from the Catalogs list, and then select **SAMPLE** from the Profiles list. Select [OK].

Select [OK] to return to the SQL QUERY TABLES window and to complete the switch to the new profile. The new profile displays only the tables that are in the sample library.

See "Setting Your Profile" on page 69 for more information about the SQL Query Window user profile.

Performing Simple Queries

Selecting a Table

First, you will analyze the relation between salary level, position, and hire date. Select **SAMPLE.SALARY** from the Available Tables list.

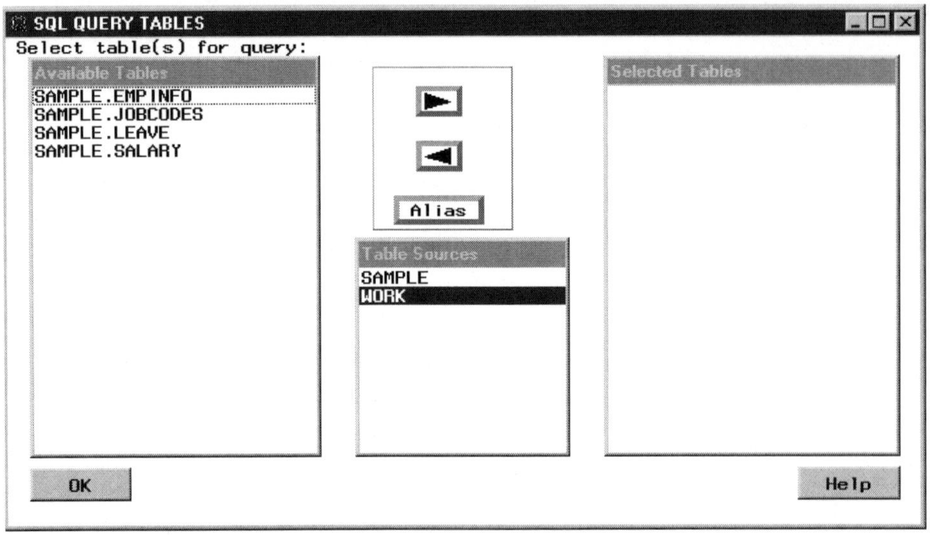

Select the right arrow to add your selection to the Selected Tables list. For mouse-enabled operating environments, you can also double-click on **SAMPLE.SALARY** to move it to the Selected Tables list. Select OK to display the SQL QUERY COLUMNS window.

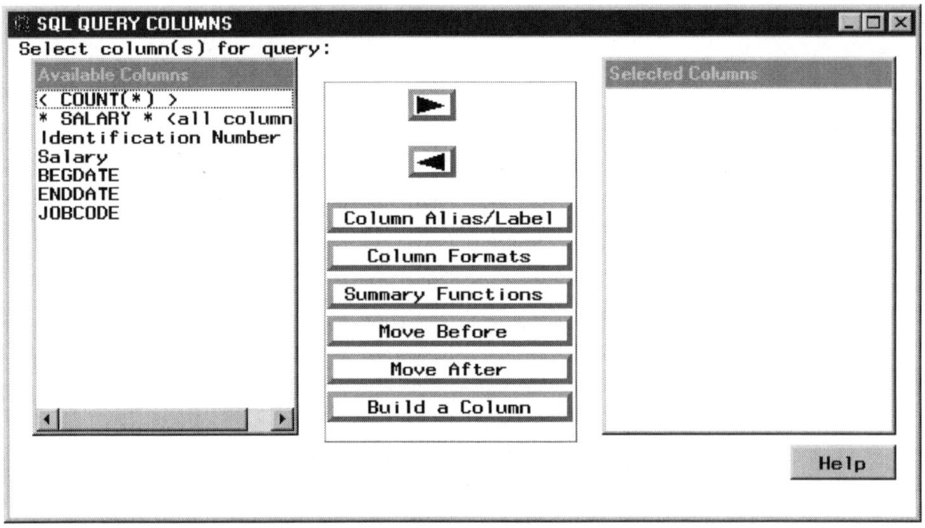

Selecting Columns

Select **Salary**, **BEGDATE**, and **JOBCODE** from the Available Columns list. Select the right arrow to add your selections to the Selected Columns list.

Alias Names and Labels

To create more descriptive labels for JOBCODE and BEGDATE, select **JOBCODE** from the Selected Columns list. Select [Column Alias/Label] to assign a new label to the JOBCODE column.

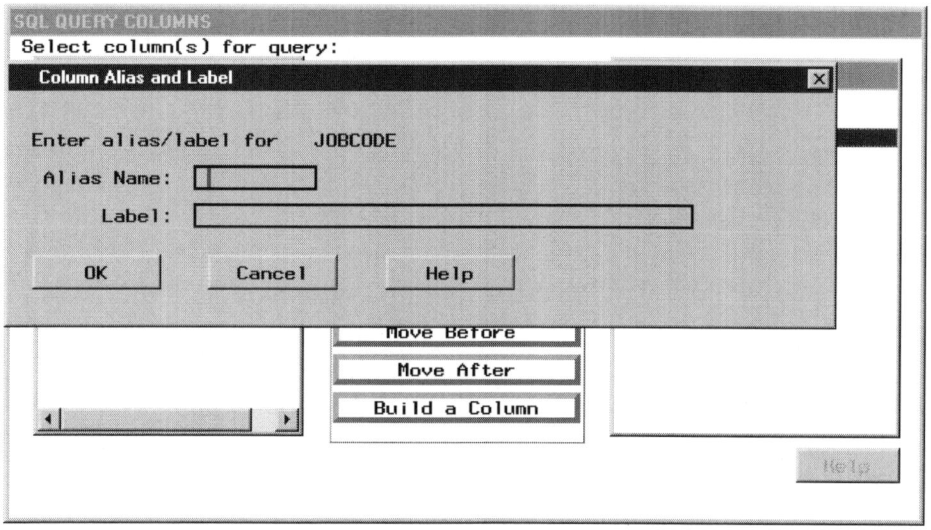

Alias Name
: specifies an alias for the column. The alias is used in place of the column name both in the query and in any table or view that is created from the query. Aliases make a result table clearer or easier to read. You can also use an alias to name a column expression.

Label
: associates a label with a column heading.

Type **Job Code** in the Label field. Select [OK] to return to the SQL QUERY COLUMNS window. The assigned label is displayed next to **JOBCODE** in the Selected Columns List.

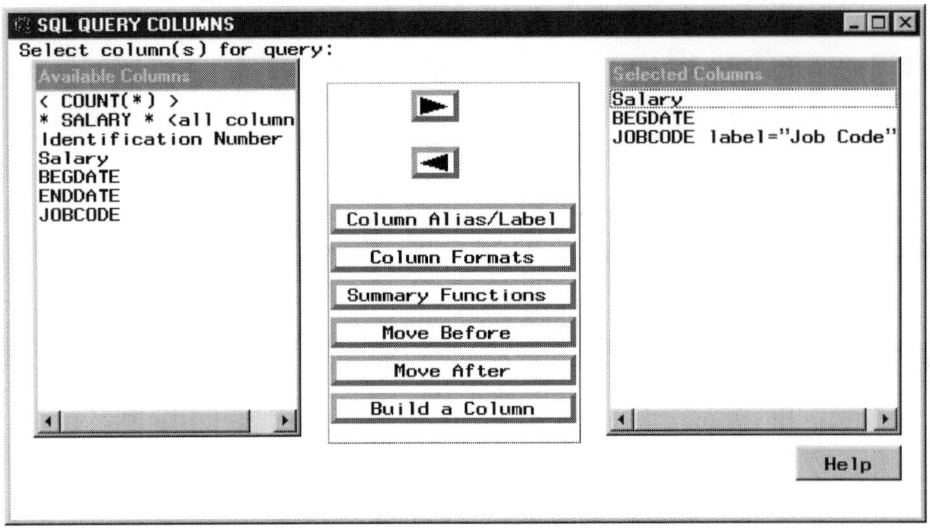

Select **BEGDATE** from the Selected Columns list. Select [Column Alias/Label]. Type **Beginning Date** in the Label field. Select [OK].

Column Format

To modify the format of the BEGDATE column, select **BEGDATE** from the Selected Columns list. Select [Column Formats] to specify the format in which the beginning dates are presented.

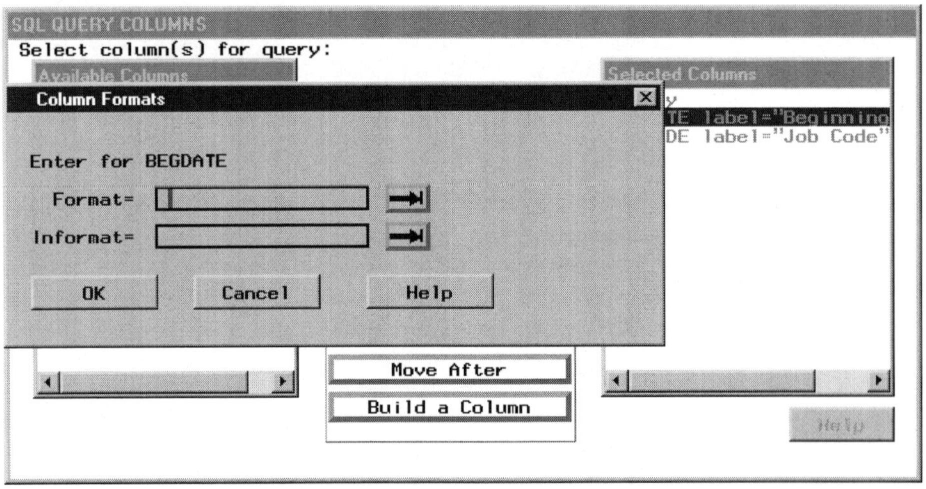

Format
: specifies the form in which the column data is displayed. You can enter a format, or select the right arrow to see a list of valid formats. When you select a format, a formatted example appears, along with its width range, default width, default decimal, and name. You can either accept the default width and decimal values, or you can specify your own values in the Width field.

Informat
: specifies the form in which the column data is read by other SAS procedures if you create a table or view from the query. You can enter an informat, or you can select

the right arrow to see a list of valid informats. When you select an informat, a formatted example appears, along with its width range, default width, default decimal, and name. You can either accept the default width and decimal values, or specify your own values.

Select the right arrow next to the Format field to display a list of formats.

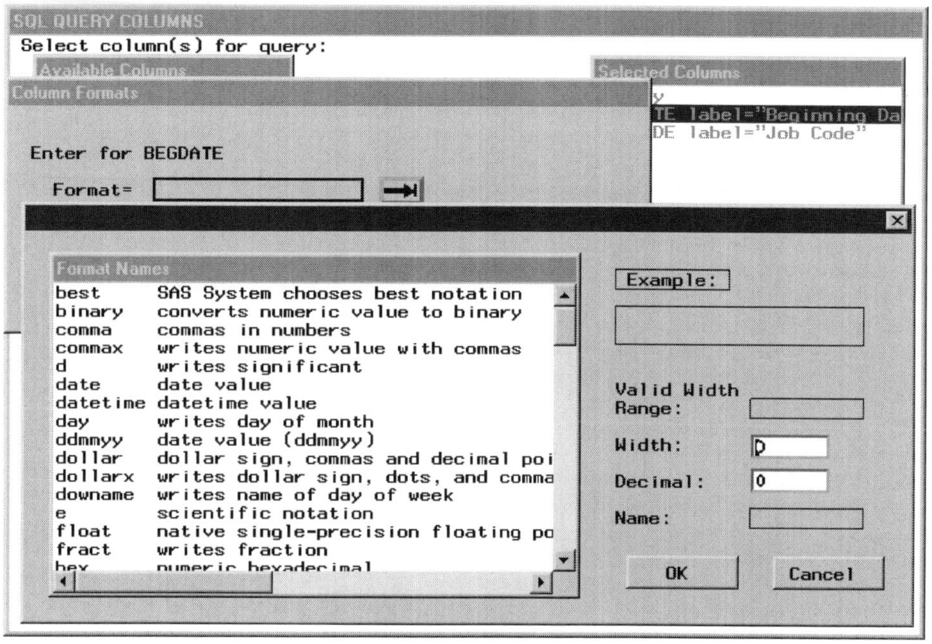

Select **date** from the Format Names list. Type **9** in the Width field. Select [OK]. Select [OK] to return to the SQL QUERY COLUMNS window.

Creating a WHERE Expression

A WHERE expression returns a subset of data that meets conditions that you specify. In this example, you create a WHERE expression that displays the range of job codes for employees who were hired after October 1991 and whose salaries are less than $18,000.00.

Select **View ▶ Where Conditions for Subset**. The WHERE EXPRESSION window appears.

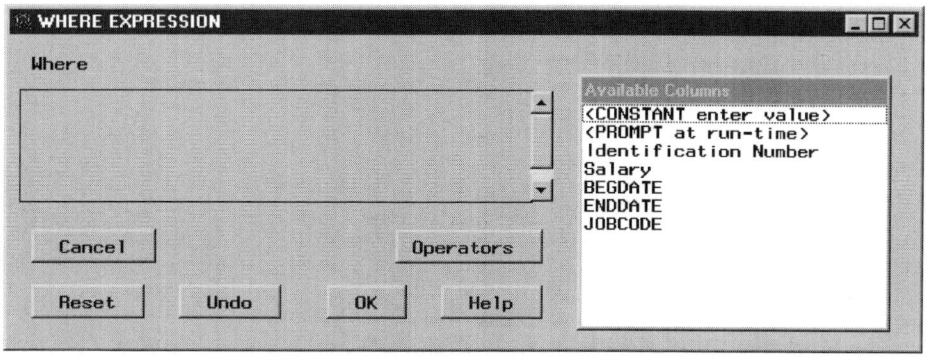

Available Columns

The Available Columns list contains all columns from the selected tables, in addition to the following choices:

<CONSTANT enter value> enables you to enter a constant value for the WHERE expression.

<PROMPT at run-time> enables you to enter a value for the WHERE expression when you run the query or create a table or view.

Comparison Operators

Select **Salary** from the Available Columns list. A list of numeric comparison operators appears.

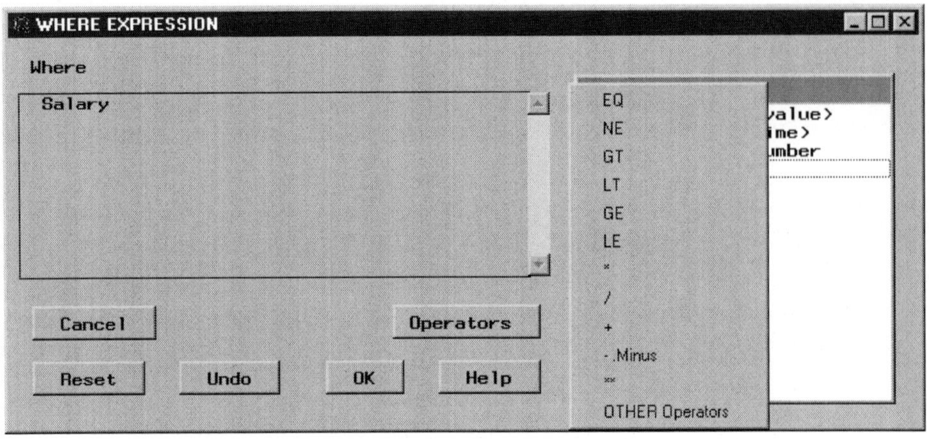

The list of operators is specific to the data type.

EQ	is equal to
NE	is not equal to
GT	is greater than
LT	is less than
GE	is greater than or equal to
LE	is less than or equal to
*	multiplies by
/	divides by
+	adds
-	subtracts
**	raises to a power

The OTHER Operators are

Is Missing	selects rows in which a column value is missing or null.
Is Not Missing	selects rows in which a column value is not missing or is not null.
Between	searches for values that lie within the specified parameters.
Not Between	searches for values that lie outside the specified parameters.

In	tests if the column value is a member of a set.
Not In	tests if the column value is not a member of a set.

Select **LT** from the list of comparison operators.

Constant Values

Select **<CONSTANT enter value>**. Enter **10000** in the Numeric field.

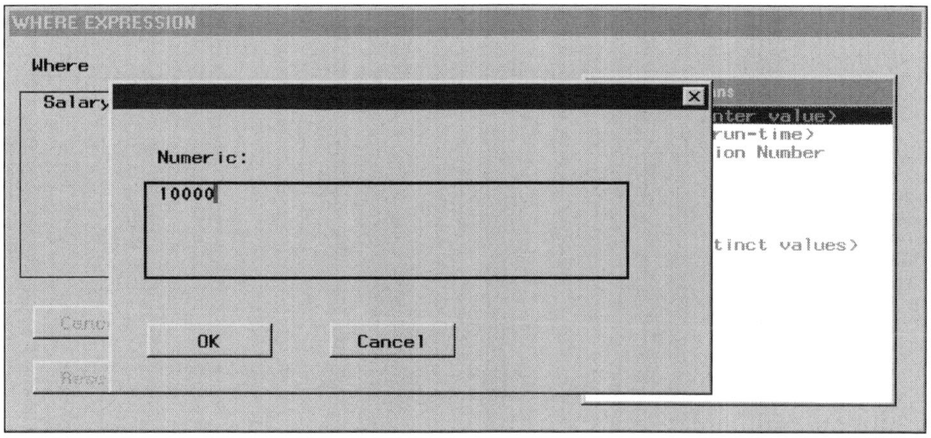

Select [OK]. The WHERE expression is built for you as you select new operators and values.

Undo

You can delete the last operator or operand that you added to the WHERE statement by selecting [Undo]. For this example, select [Undo] to remove **10000** from the WHERE statement.

Lookup Distinct Values

Select **<LOOKUP distinct values>** to view all the unique values that exist in the SALARY column.

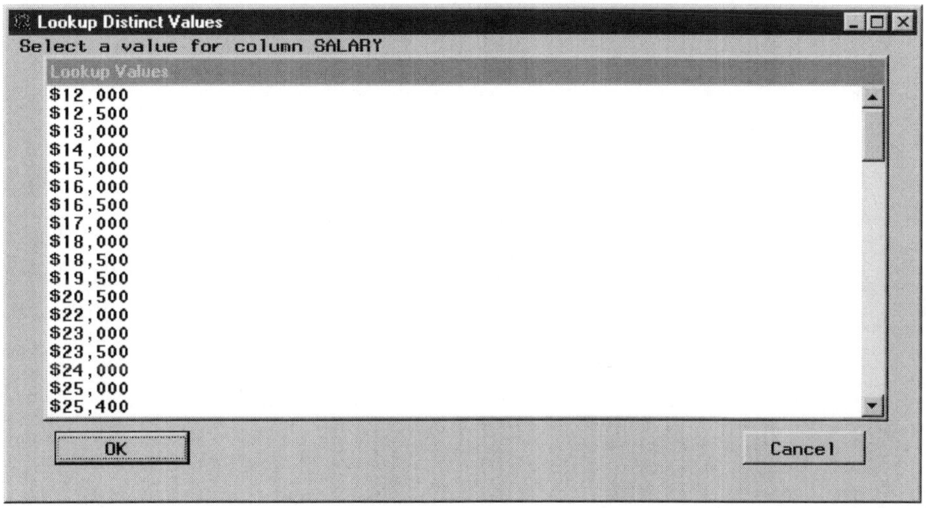

Select **$18,000** from the list of values. Because the LT comparison operator requires only one value, the WHERE EXPRESSION window automatically reappears.

Logical Operators

Select [Operators] to display the list of operators. Note that the list of comparison operators has changed to a list of logical operators. Select **AND** from the list of operators.

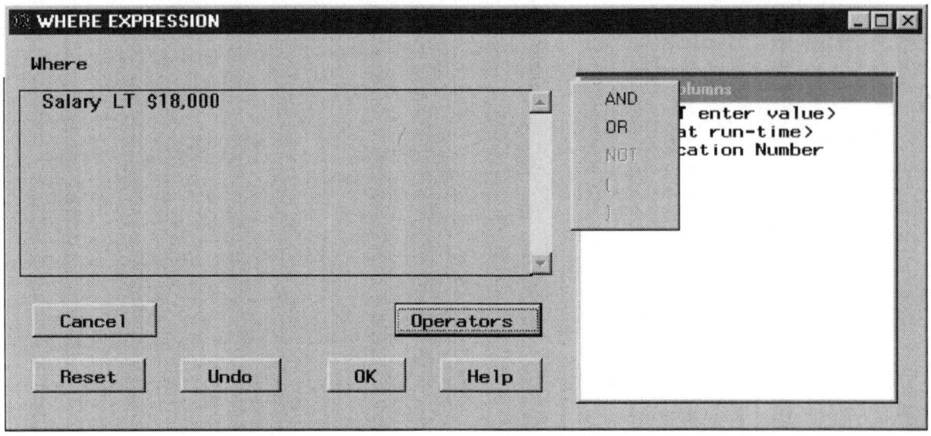

Select **BEGDATE** from the Available Columns list. Select **GT** from the list of comparison operators.

Run-Time Prompt

Select **<PROMPT at run-time>** to display the Prompt String dialog box. Type **Beginning Date:** in the Prompt String field.

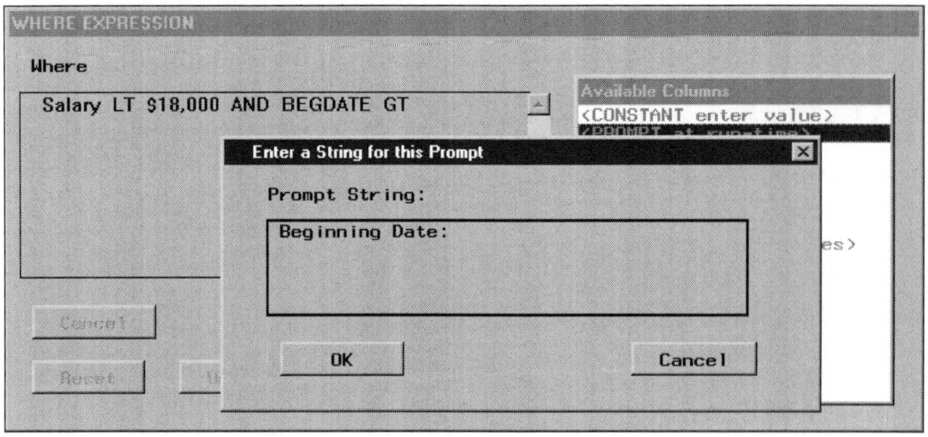

Select [OK]. **&PROMPT1** in the WHERE expression indicates that you will supply a value for this variable when you run the query.

Select [OK] from the WHERE EXPRESSION window to return to the SQL QUERY COLUMNS window.

Running Your Query

To run your query, select **Tools ▶ Run Query ▶ Run Immediate**.

The Prompt at Run Time window appears, with the **`Beginning Date:`** prompt that you specified in the WHERE expression.

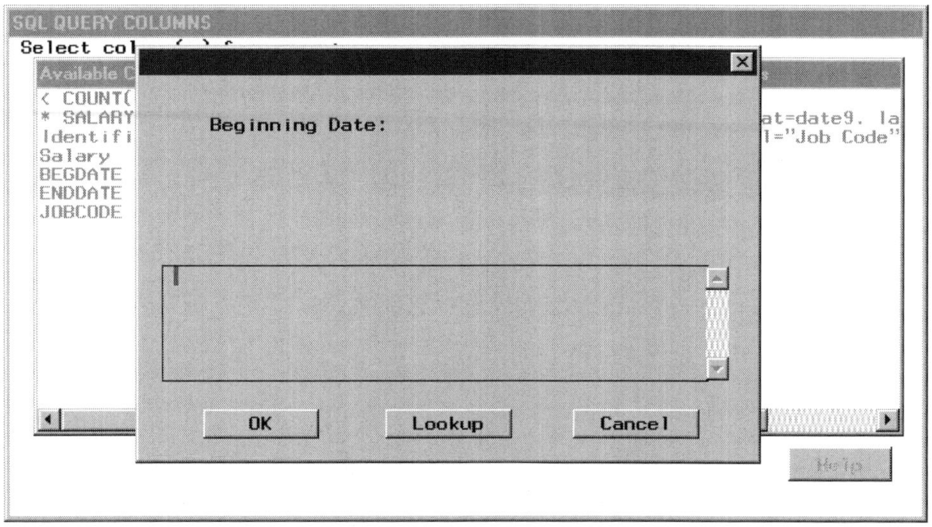

Select [Lookup] to display a list of values for the BEGDATE column.

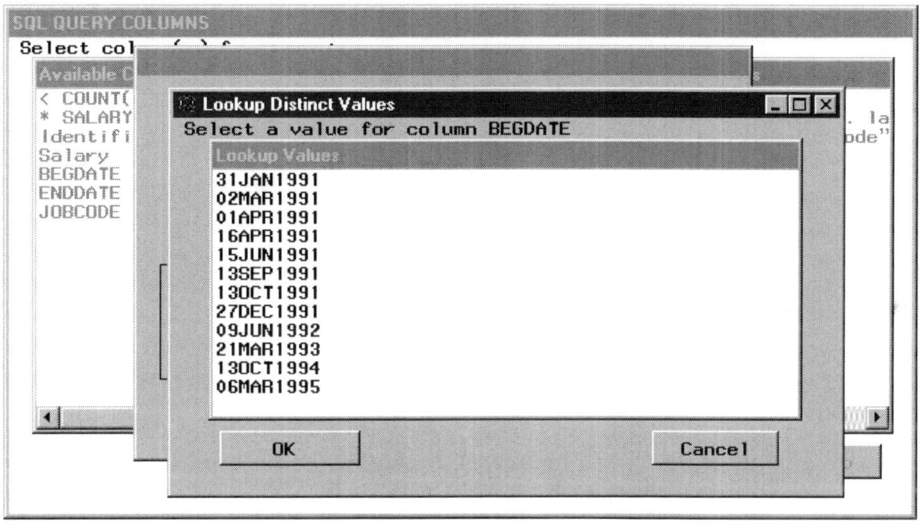

Select **`13OCT1991`** from the list of values; the Prompt at Run Time window is displayed with the value that you selected. Select [OK] to continue to run the query and to view your output in the Output window.

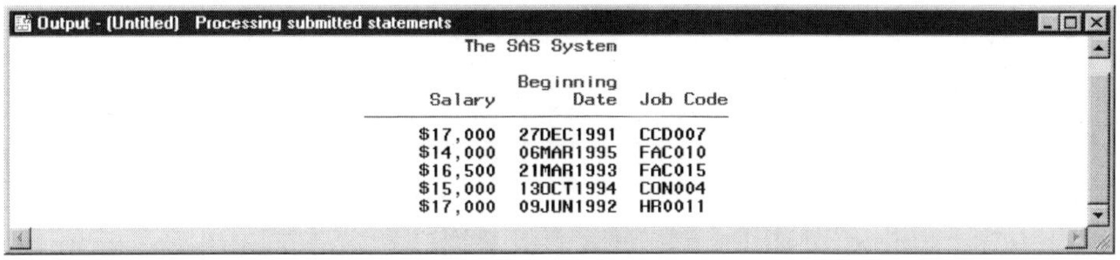

Sorting Your Output

You can specify the order in which you want the output sorted. In this example, you use the query from the last example and change the ordering sequence of the columns in the Output window. From the SQL QUERY COLUMNS window, select **View ▶ Order By**.

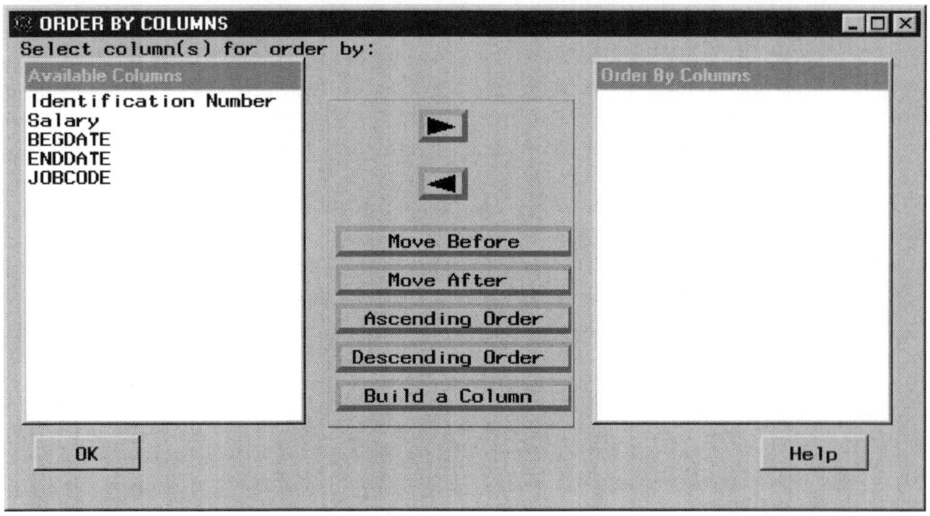

`Move Before` displays all columns in the Order By Columns list except the currently chosen one. The currently chosen column will be inserted before the column that you select.

`Move After` displays all the columns in the Order By Columns list except the currently chosen one. The currently chosen column will be inserted following the column that you select.

`Ascending Order` changes the ordering sequence of the selected column's values to ascending (lowest value to highest value).

`Descending Order` changes the ordering sequence of the selected column's values to descending.

`Build a Column` displays the Build a Column Expression window, which enables you to create a calculated column for use in sorting your output. Use the Build a Column Expression window to create new columns by performing calculations on existing (numeric) columns.

Order By Columns

Select **`BEGDATE`** from the Available Columns list. Select the right arrow to move the column to the Order By Columns list. By default, columns are sorted in ascending order, so the abbreviation ASC appears next to the column name in the Order By Columns list. Select **`BEGDATE ASC`** and [Descending Order] to change the ordering sequence.

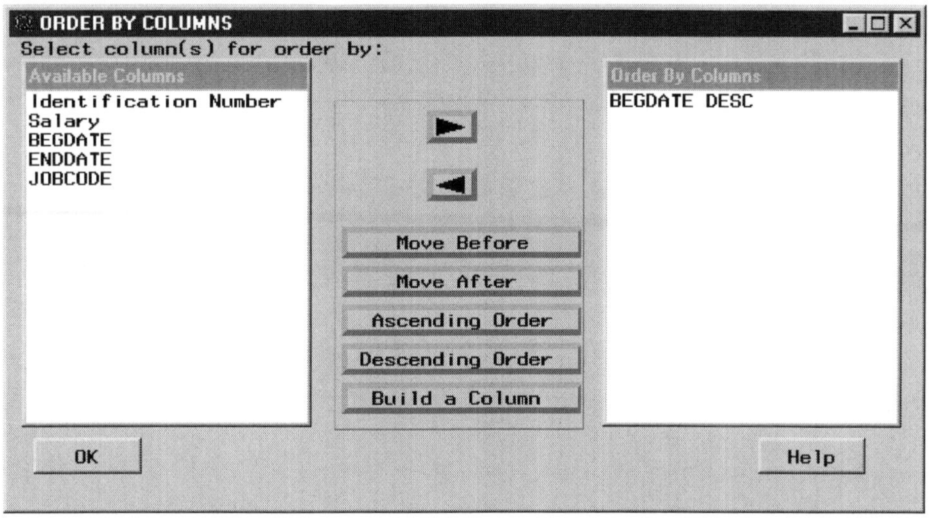

Select **Salary** and **JOBCODE**, and move them to the Order By Columns list.

Move Columns

Select **Salary ASC** from the Order By Columns list and select [Move Before]. The Move Columns window appears.

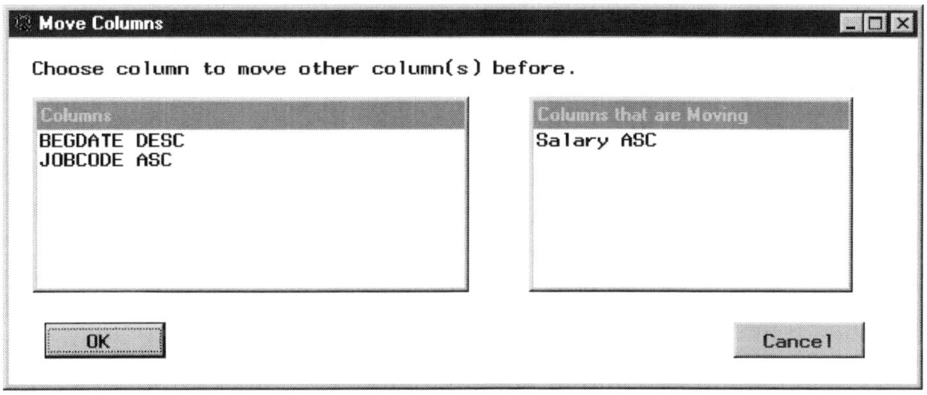

Select **BEGDATE** and [OK]. The ORDER BY COLUMNS window appears with **Salary** first in the Order By Columns list.

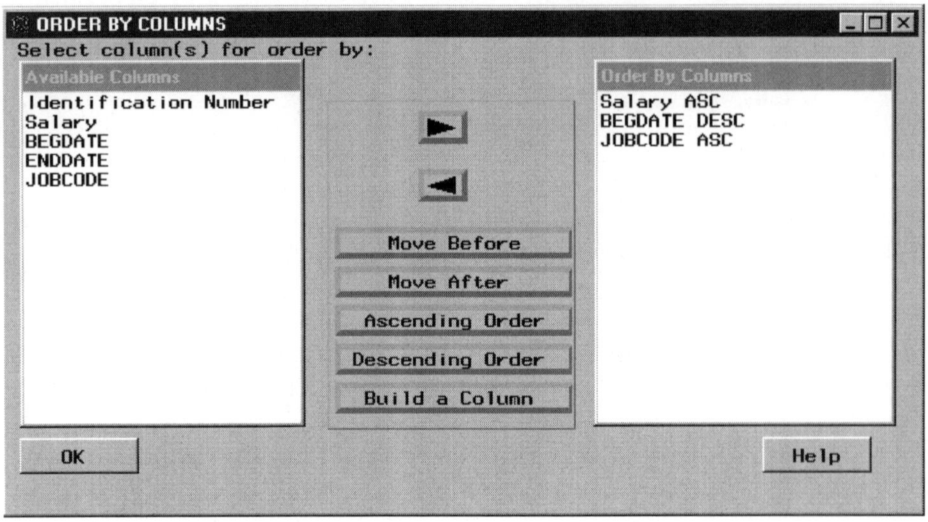

Select OK to return to the SQL QUERY COLUMNS window.

Select **View ▶ Where Conditions for Subset**.

The WHERE EXPRESSION window appears. Select Undo four times, until only **`SALARY LT $18,000`** is displayed.

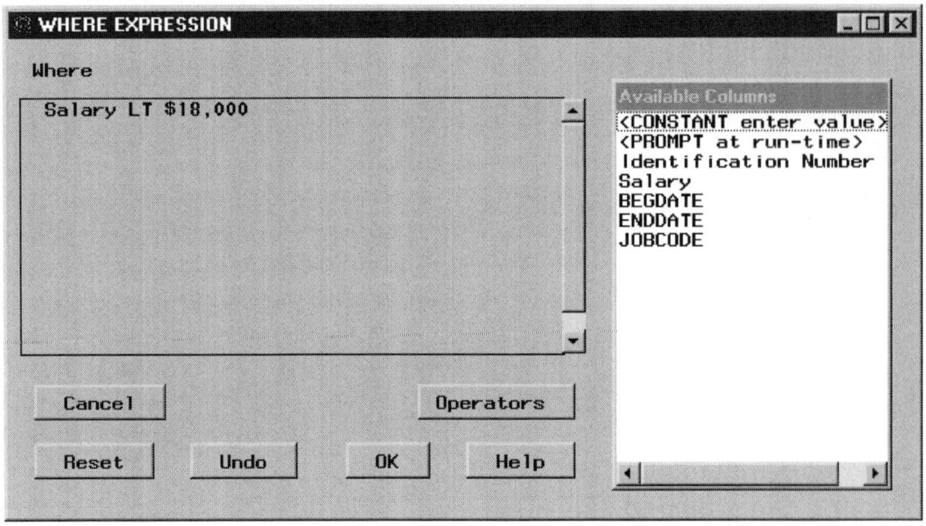

Select OK.

Viewing Your Output

To run your query and view the output in the Output window, select **Tools ▶ Run Query ▶ Run Immediate**.

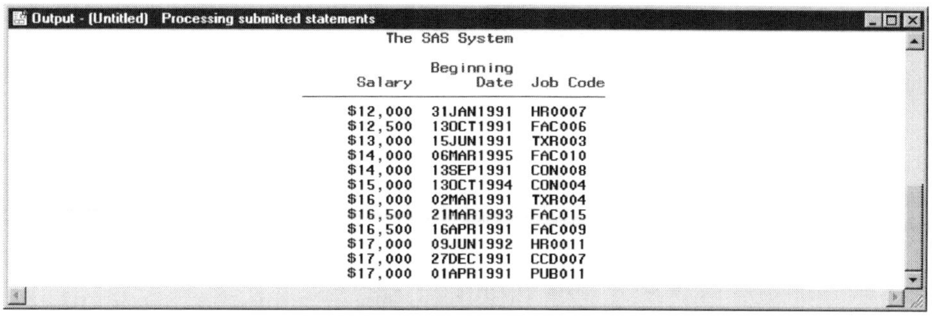

Building Calculated Columns

Using the query from the last example, you can create a new column that computes the hourly wage for each salary.

Build a Column Expression

Select [Build a Column] from the SQL QUERY COLUMNS window to display the BUILD A COLUMN EXPRESSION window.

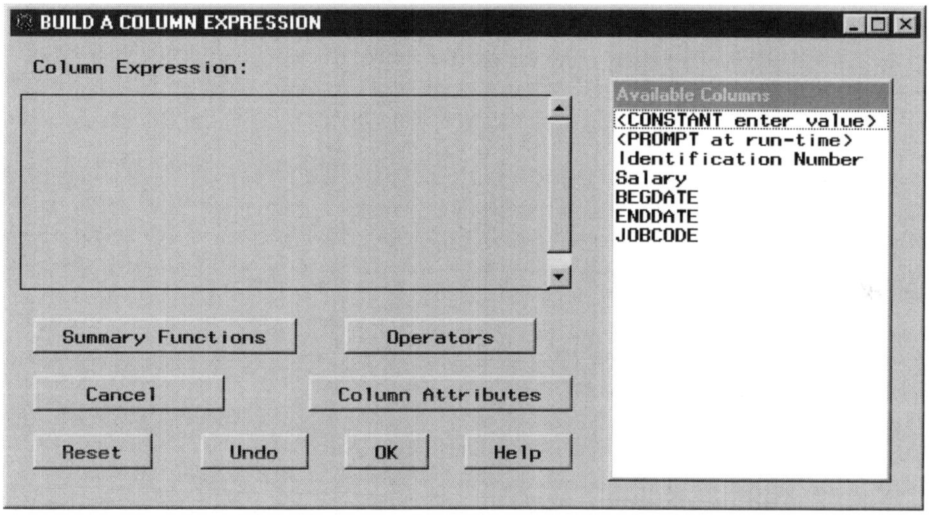

Select **Salary** from the Available Columns list. Select the division operator (/) from the list of operators.

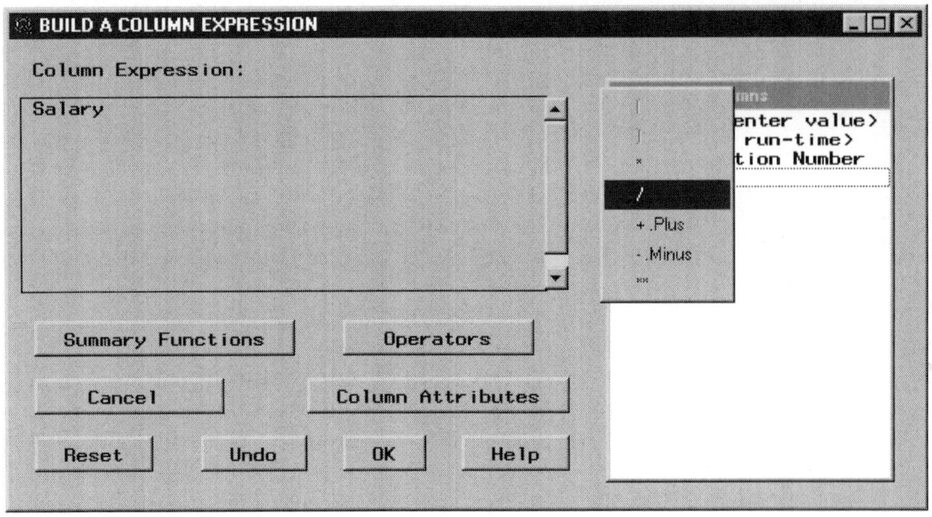

Select **<CONSTANT enter value>** from the Available Columns list. Enter **50** in the Numeric Constant dialog box. Select [OK] to return to the BUILD A COLUMN EXPRESSION window.

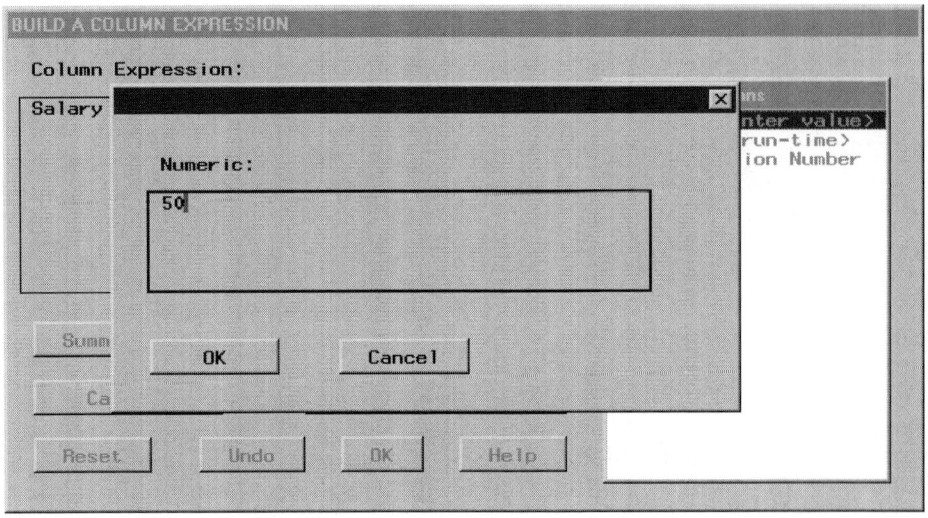

Select the division operator again from the list of operators. Select **<CONSTANT enter value>** and enter **40** to divide the number of weeks by the number of hours in each week. Select [OK]. Select outside the list of operators to dismiss it.

Correcting Your Mistakes

You realize that you have made a mistake and that you want to divide Salary by 52, the number of weeks in a year. Select **50** in the Column Expression field. A pop-up menu displays a list of choices.

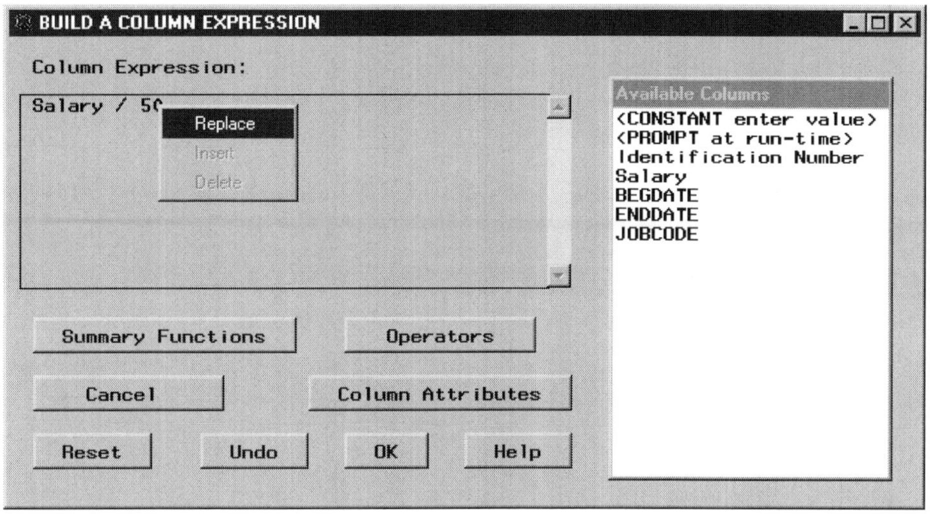

Select **`Replace`** from the pop-up menu. The BUILD A COLUMN EXPRESSION window displays **`Select from Available Columns to replace this value`**.

Select **`<CONSTANT enter value>`** from the Available Columns list. Enter **`52`** as the new constant and select [OK].

Defining the Column Format and Label

Select [Column Attributes] to define the format and label for your new column.

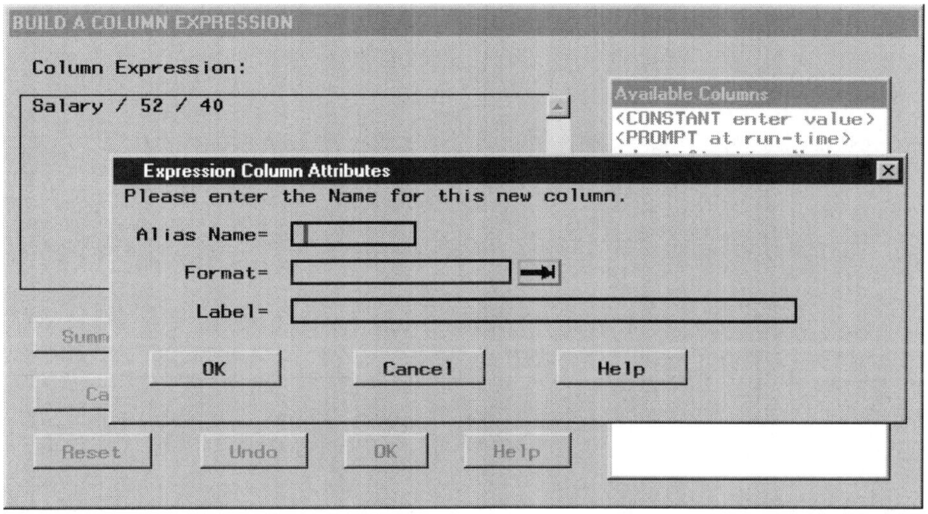

Enter **`hourly`** as the alias name. Select the right arrow next to the Format field to choose the format in which the new column will appear.

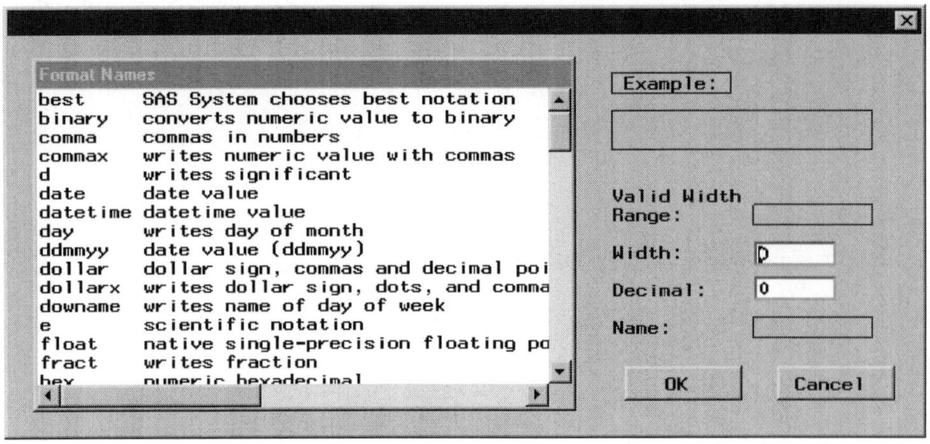

Select **`dollar`** from the Format Names list. Enter **`2`** in the Decimal field so that the hourly wage will be displayed to two decimal places. Select OK.

Enter **`Hourly Rate`** in the Label field for the column. Select OK.

The complete calculated column is displayed in the BUILD A COLUMN EXPRESSION window.

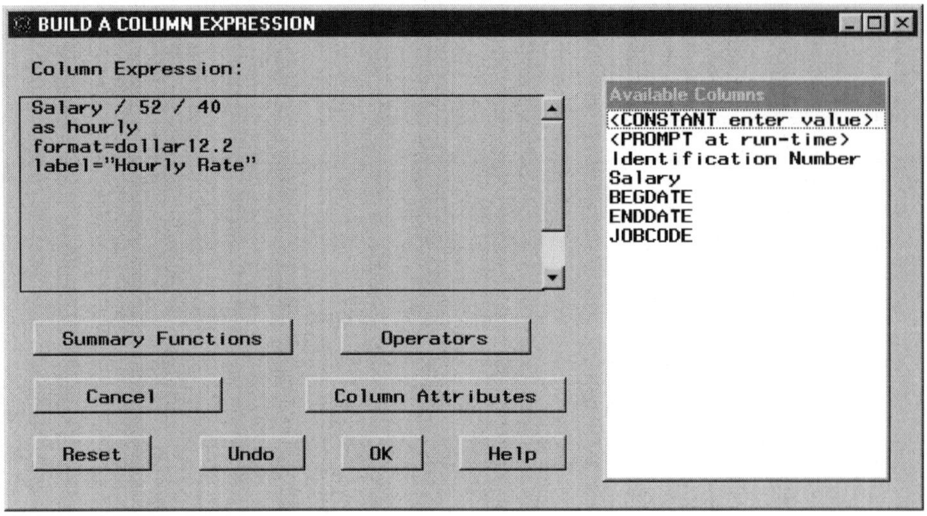

Select **`OK`** to return to the SQL QUERY COLUMNS window. Note that the new column has automatically been added to the Selected Columns list.

Viewing Your Output

To run your query and view the output in the Output window, select **Tools ▸ Run Query ▸ Run Immediate**.

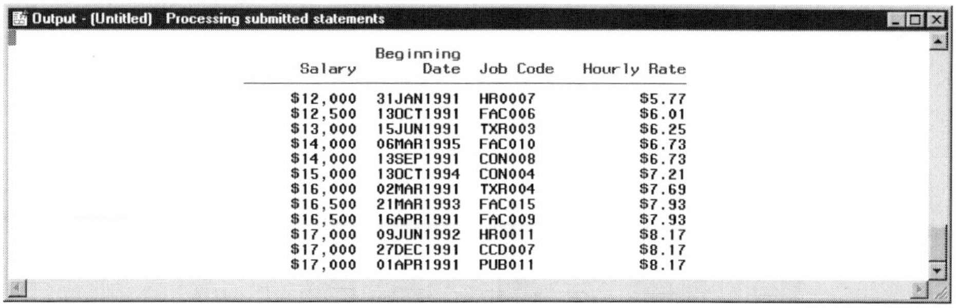

Salary	Beginning Date	Job Code	Hourly Rate
$12,000	31JAN1991	HR0007	$5.77
$12,500	13OCT1991	FAC006	$6.01
$13,000	15JUN1991	TXR003	$6.25
$14,000	06MAR1995	FAC010	$6.73
$14,000	13SEP1991	CON008	$6.73
$15,000	13OCT1994	CON004	$7.21
$16,000	02MAR1991	TXR004	$7.69
$16,500	21MAR1993	FAC015	$7.93
$16,500	16APR1991	FAC009	$7.93
$17,000	09JUN1992	HR0011	$8.17
$17,000	27DEC1991	CCD007	$8.17
$17,000	01APR1991	PUB011	$8.17

Building and Adding Tables

Using the query from the last example, you can build a new table from the results.

Creating a Table from Query Results

In the SQL QUERY COLUMNS window, select **View ▸ Tables** to return to the SQL QUERY TABLES window.

From the SQL QUERY TABLES window, select **File ▸ Create Table from Query Results**.

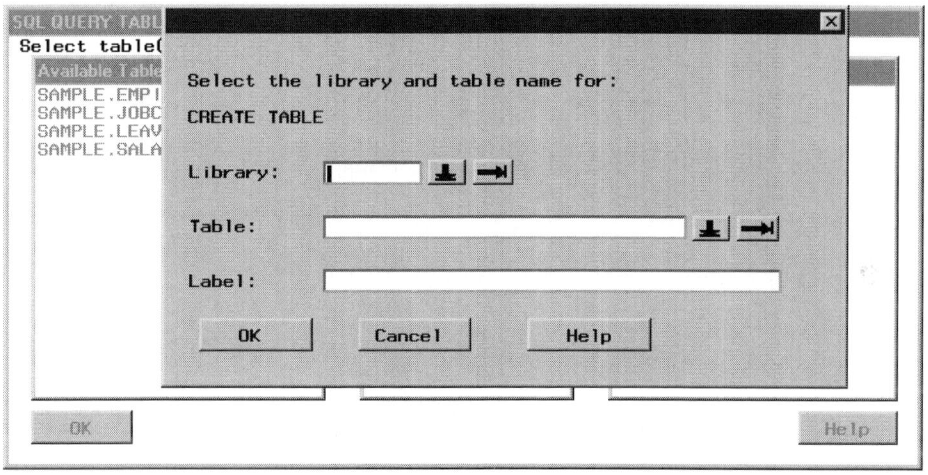

Select the right arrow next to the Library field to display a list of available libraries.

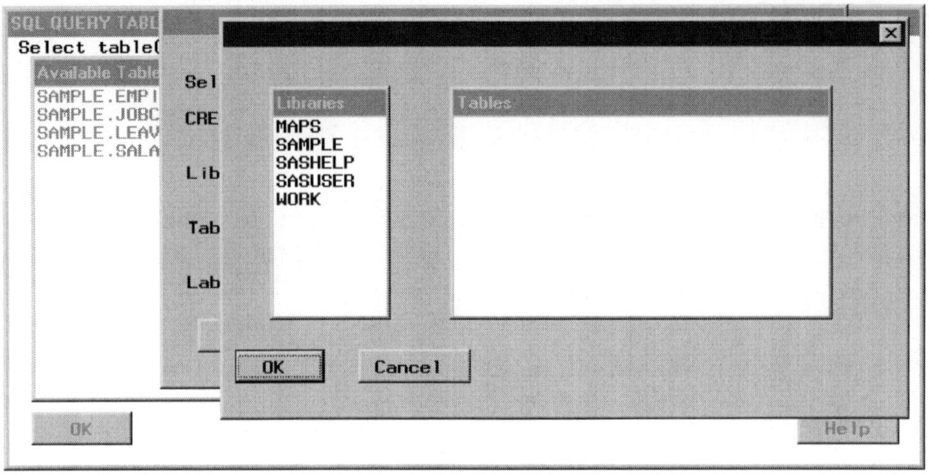

You can also type the library name in the Library field.
Select **SAMPLE** to include your new table in the SAMPLE library.

Note: If you do not have write access to the SAMPLE library, then select **SASUSER** instead. △

Select [OK].
Type **WAGE** in the Table field.
Type **Hourly Wages** in the Label field.
Select [OK] to return to the SQL QUERY TABLES window.
Select **Tools ▸ Reset** to reset your query. Select [OK] from the dialog box that appears. Note that SAMPLE.WAGE is now in the Available Tables list.

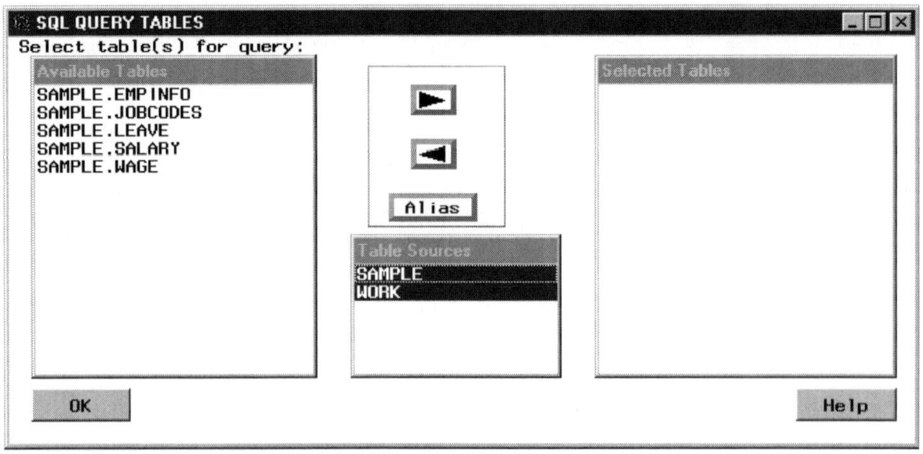

Joining Matching Data

The data that you need for a report could be located in more than one table. In order to select the data from the tables, you *join* the tables in a query. Joining tables enables you to select data from multiple tables as if the data were contained in one table. Joins do not alter the original tables.

The SQL Query Window supports two types of joins:

- *Inner Joins* return a result table for all the rows in a table that have one or more matching rows in the other table or tables that are listed in the Selected Tables list.

- *Outer Joins* are inner joins that are augmented with rows that do not match any row from the other table in the join. See "Creating and Using Outer Joins" on page 64 for more information about outer joins.

For this example, you use an inner join to display the hourly wage for each employee identification number.

In the previous example, you added SAMPLE.WAGE to the Available Tables list. Select SAMPLE.SALARY and SAMPLE.WAGE from the Available Tables list and add them to the Selected Tables list. Select [OK] to display the SQL QUERY COLUMNS window.

Select **`Identification Number`**, **`JOBCODE`**, and **`Hourly Rate`** from the Available Columns list and move them to the Selected Columns list.

Choosing a Join Type

Select **View ▸ Join Type** to display the Join Types window.

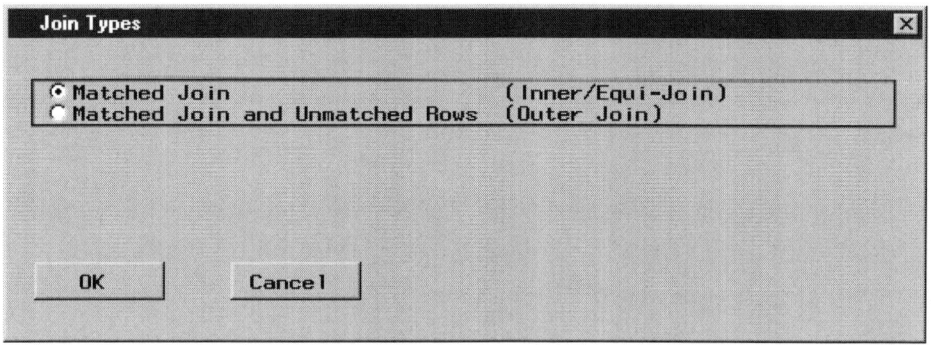

Select **`Matched Join`** and [OK].

Setting Join Criteria

In the Columns for Setting Join Criteria window, select **`Salary`** from both the SAMPLE.SALARY Columns list and the SAMPLE.WAGE Columns list. Select **`JOBCODE`** from the SAMPLE.SALARY Columns list and select **`Job Code`** from the SAMPLE.WAGE Columns list.

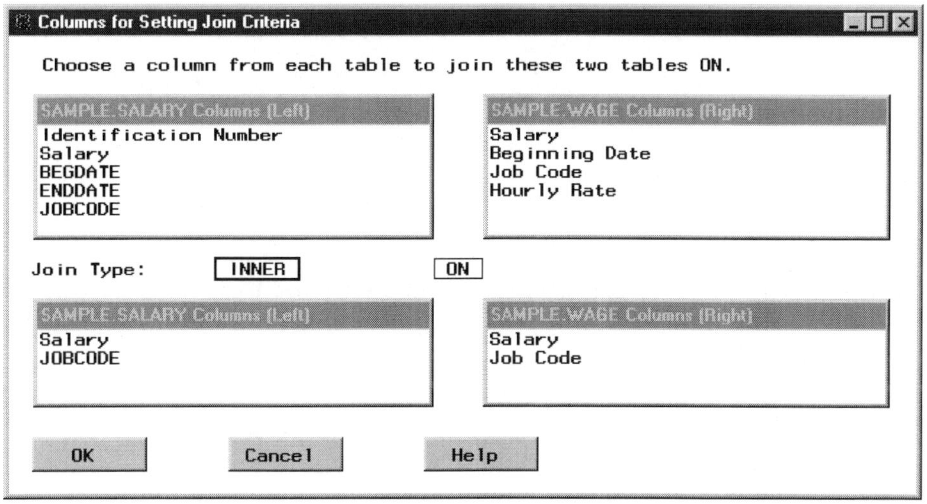

Select OK to return to the SQL QUERY COLUMNS window.

Viewing Your Output

To run your query and view the output in the Output window, select **Tools ► Run Query ► Run Immediate**.

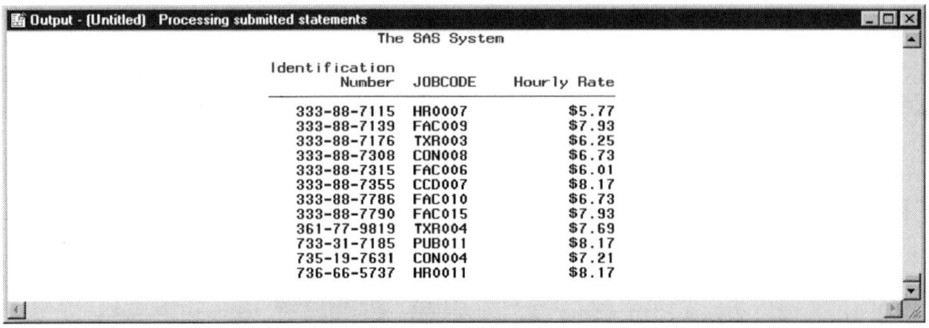

Saving Queries

To save the query that you created in the previous example in SASUSER.PROFILE, select **Tools ► Show Query** to display the SQL QUERY window.

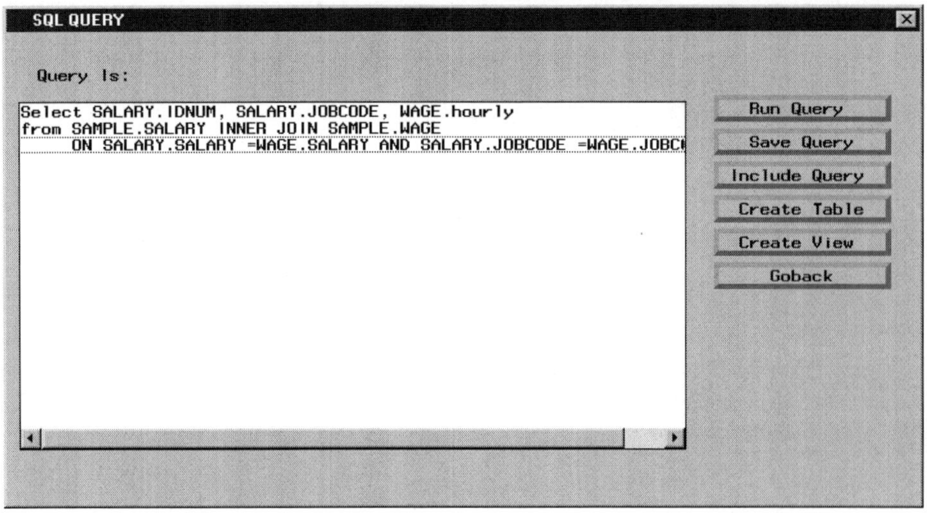

Saving a Query to Include Later

Select **Save Query ► Save as QUERY to Include later** to save your query to SASUSER.PROFILE or another catalog of your choosing.

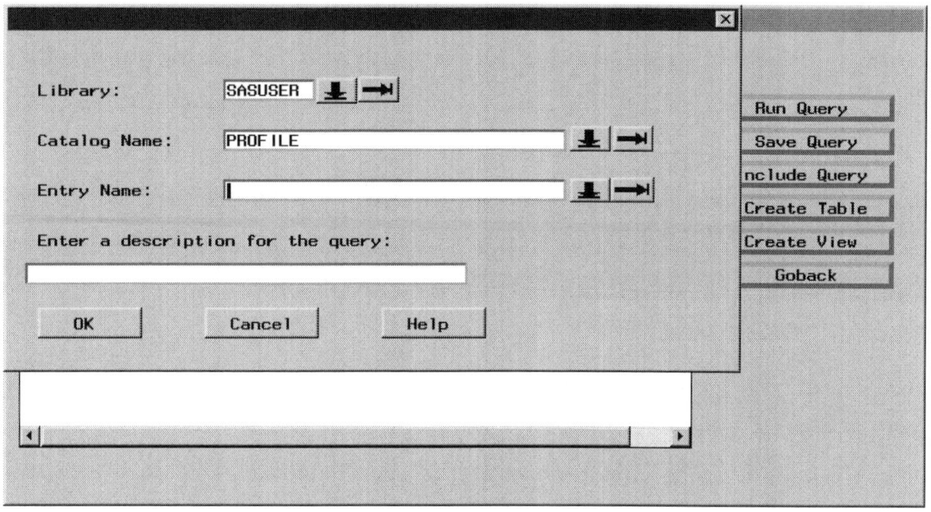

Type **`IDWAGE`** in the Entry Name field. Type **`ID number and hourly wage`** in the description field. Select [OK] to save your query as an entry in SASUSER.PROFILE and to return to the SQL QUERY window. Select [Goback] to return to the SQL QUERY COLUMNS window.

Saving Several Queries

You can save more than one query and then select from a list of queries that you have saved in the current Query Window session or in a previous Query Window session. In this example, you create and save several queries for later selection from a list of the saved queries.

From the SQL QUERY COLUMNS window, select **View ▸ Tables** to return to the SQL QUERY TABLES window.

Remove SAMPLE.WAGE from the Selected Tables list. Select [OK] to display the SQL QUERY COLUMNS window.

Select **`Salary`** from the Available Columns list and add it to the Selected Columns list. Select **View ▸ Where Conditions for Subset** to display the WHERE EXPRESSION window.

Select **`Salary`** from the Available Columns list. Select **`GT`** (greater than) from the list of operators. Select **`<LOOKUP distinct values>`** from the Available Columns list. Select **`$25,000`** from the Lookup Values window. Select [OK] to save your WHERE expression.

Select **View ▸ Order By** to display the ORDER BY COLUMNS window. Select **`Salary`** from the Available Columns list and add it to the Selected Columns list. Select [OK] to return to the SQL QUERY COLUMNS window.

In addition to the method of saving queries that was described earlier, you can also select **File ▸ Save Query ▸ Save as Query to Include later**. Type **`ABOVE25`** in the Entry Name field. Type **`Salaries above $25,000`** in the description field. Select [OK].

You can also save queries that will be processed against different tables. To create the next query that you will save, select **View ▸ Tables** to return to the SQL QUERY TABLES window. Remove **`SAMPLE.SALARY`** from the Selected Tables list. If a dialog box appears, then select [OK] to clear the WHERE expression.

Select **`SAMPLE.EMPINFO`** from the Available Tables list and add it to the Selected Tables list. Select [OK] to display the SQL QUERY COLUMNS window.

Add **`NAME`**, **`DIVISION`**, and **`Education Level`** to the Selected Columns list. Select **View ▸ Where Conditions for Subset**.

Select **`Education level`** from the Available Columns list. Select **`GE`** (greater than or equal to) from the list of operators. Select **`<LOOKUP distinct values>`**, and select **`20`** from the Lookup Values list. Select [OK] to return to the SQL QUERY COLUMNS window.

Select **File ▸ Save Query ▸ Save as Query to Include later**.

Type **`EDU20`** in the Entry Name field. Type **`Education level above 20 years`** in the description field. Select [OK] to save the query.

Listing Saved Queries

You can now display a list of the queries that you have saved, and include one of the queries. Select **File ▸ List/Include Saved Queries**. The queries that you have created are listed in the Saved Queries window.

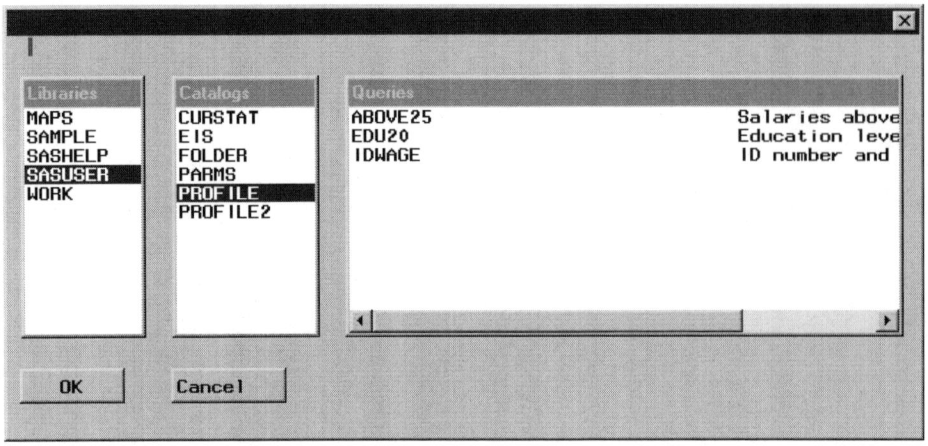

Including a Saved Query

Select **`SASUSER.PROFILE.EDU20`** and select [OK]. A dialog box asks whether you want to clear the previous query or include the previous query with the new one. Select [OK].

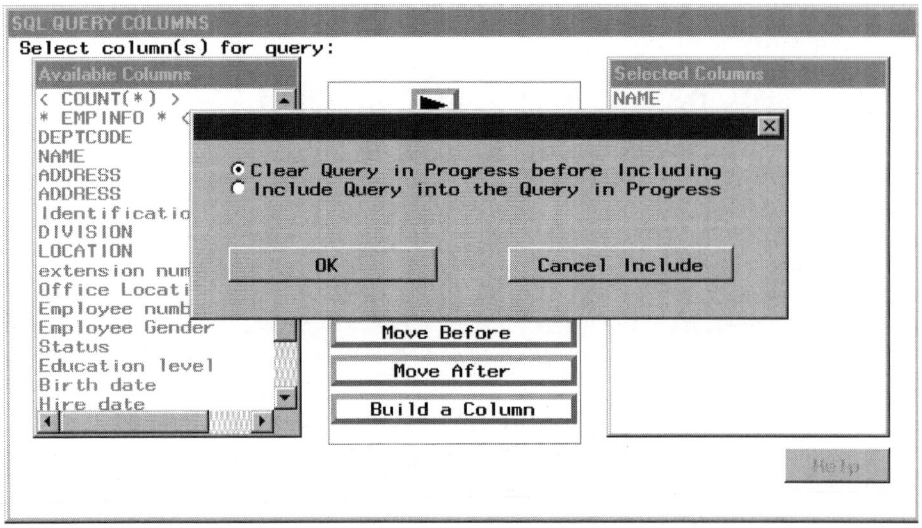

Viewing Your Output

You can run SASUSER.PROFILE.EDU20 by selecting **Tools ▶ Run Query ▶ Run Immediate**. The results are displayed in the Output window.

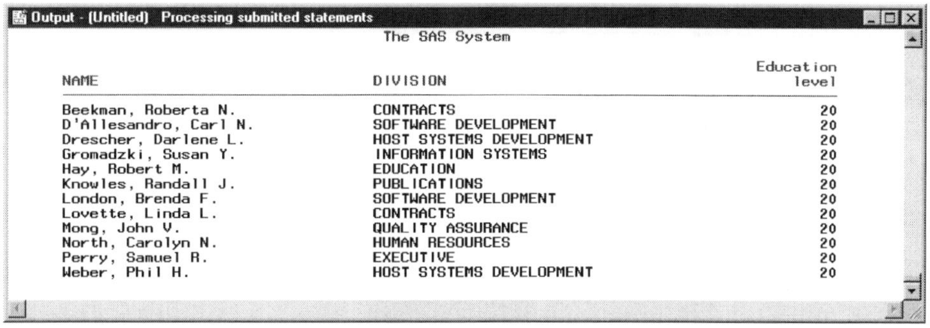

Using Parentheses and Other Operators

You can use operators other than the comparison operators to subset your data for querying; you can easily change a WHERE condition that has been previously set.

Changing a WHERE Expression

You can change the WHERE expression in SASUSER.PROFILE.EDU20 from the previous example. In the SQL QUERY TABLES window, select **View ▶ Where Conditions for Subset**.

Select [Operators] to display the list of valid operators.

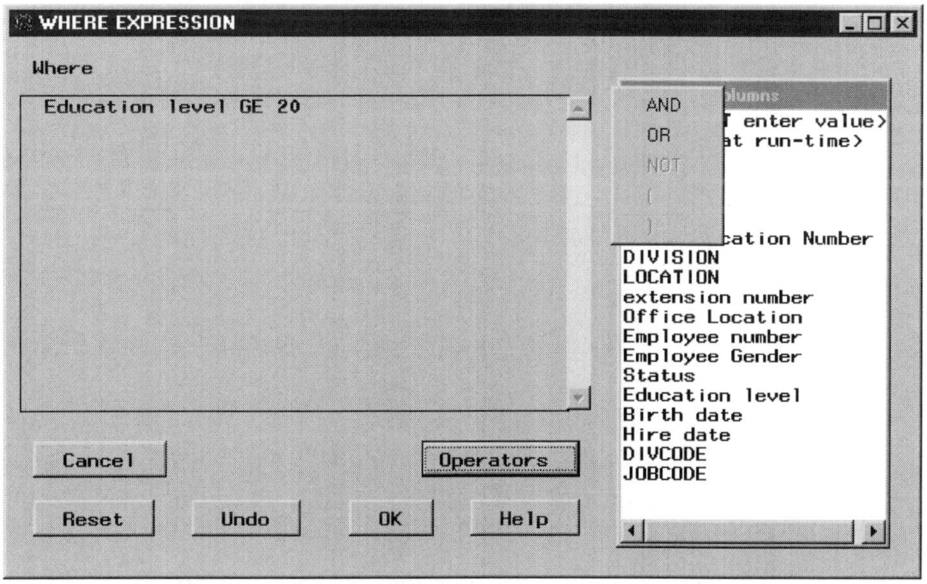

AND

Select **AND** from the list.

Select [Operators]. Select **(** from the list. Select **Birth date** from the Available Columns list. Select **OTHER Operators** from the list of operators to display a second menu of operators.

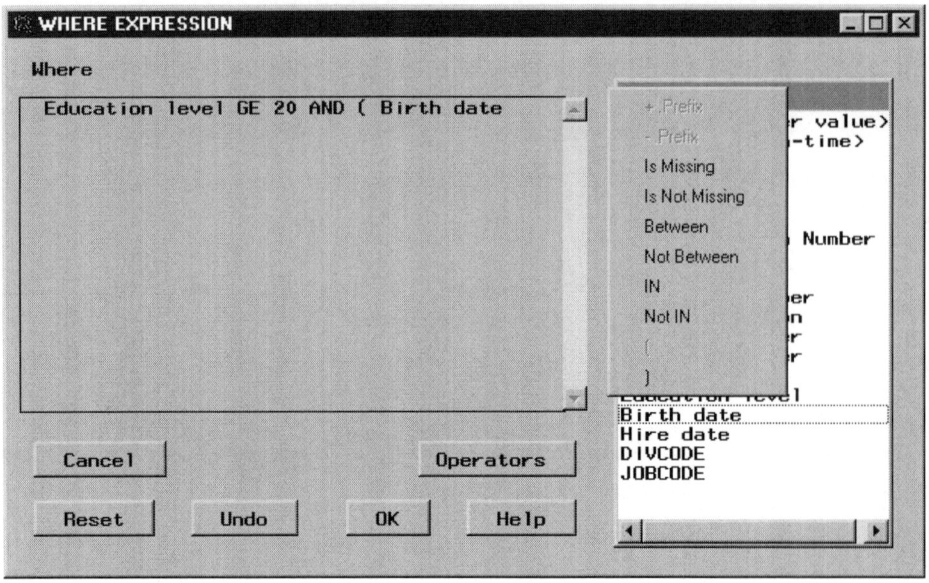

Between

Select **Between** from the list of other operators.
Select **<LOOKUP distinct values>** from the Available Columns list.

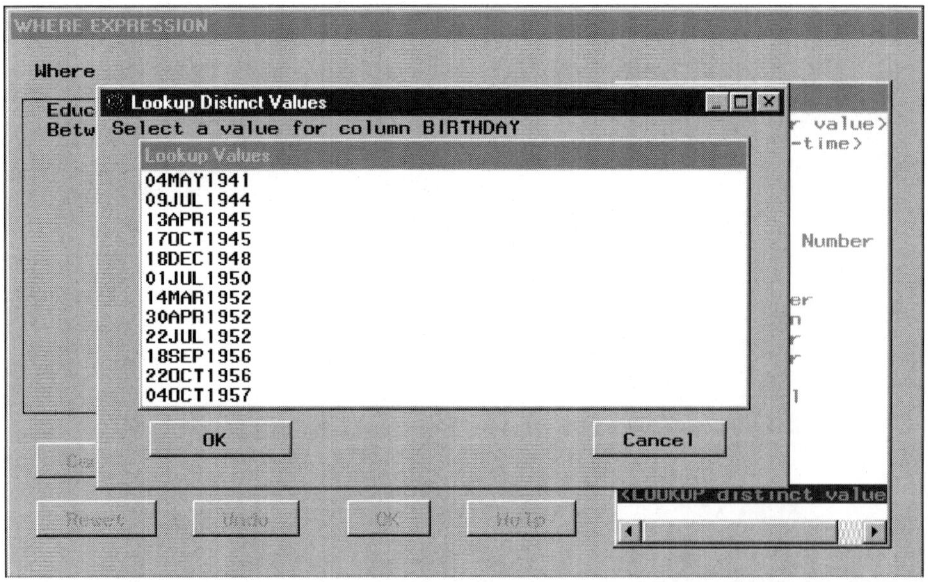

Select **17OCT1945** from the Lookup Values list. Because the Between operator requires a second value, the Lookup Distinct Values window appears again after you select a value. Select **18DEC1948** from the Lookup Values list.

In the WHERE EXPRESSION window, select [Operators]. Select **)** from the list of operators to complete the expression that will be evaluated first when the query is run.

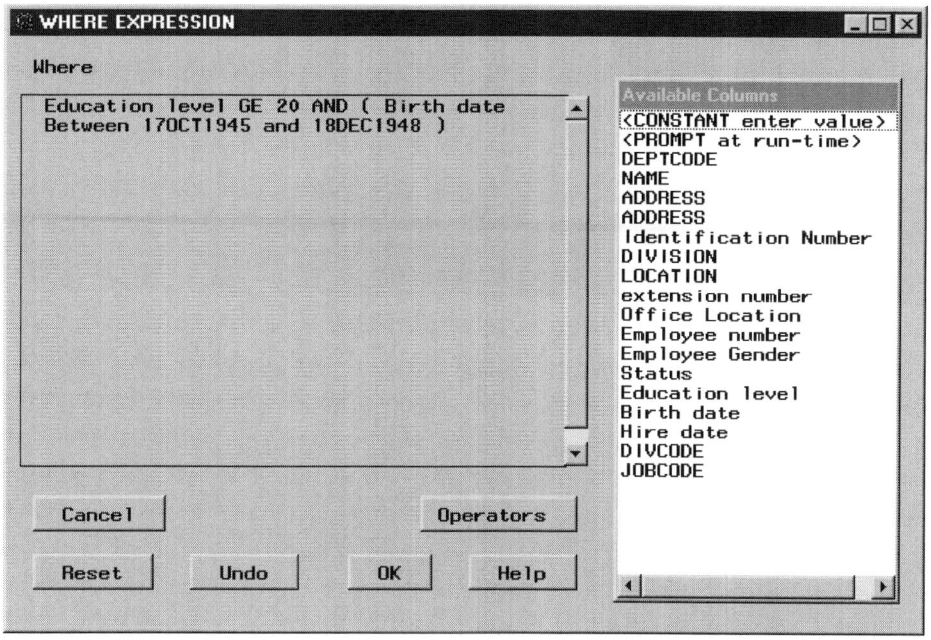

Select OK to return to the SQL QUERY COLUMNS window.

Viewing Your Output

Select **Tools ▶ Run Query ▶ Run Immediate** to display the output of your query.

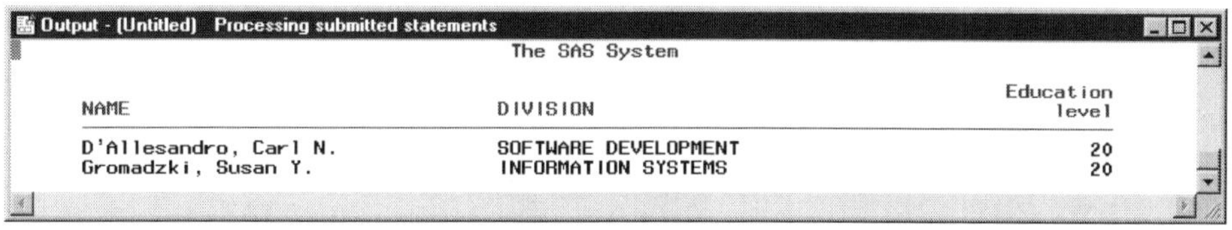

From the SQL QUERY COLUMNS window, select **Tools ▶ Reset** to reset your query.

Designing and Saving a Report

When you run your query, you can use the REPORT procedure to modify your output.

If there is an active query in the SQL Query Window, then select **Tools ▶ Reset** to clear the query. Select OK in the dialog box that appears.

In the SQL QUERY TABLES window, select **SAMPLE.EMPINFO** and **SAMPLE.SALARY** from the Available Tables list and add them to the Selected Tables list.

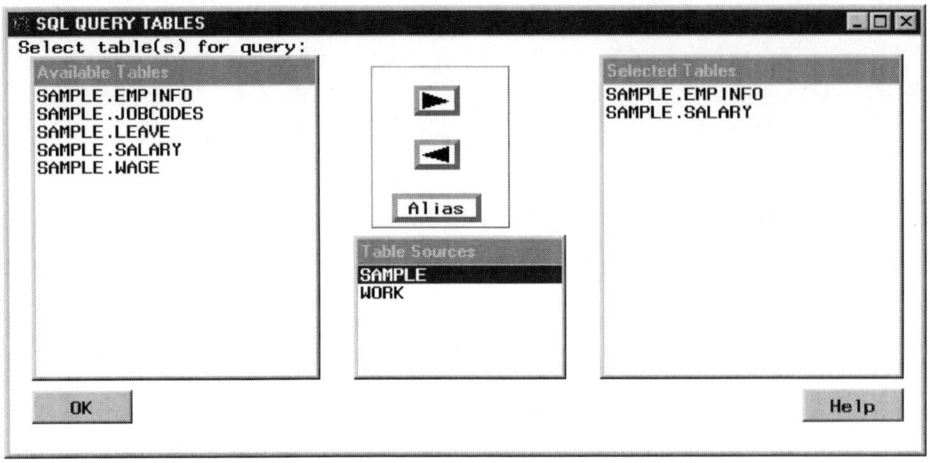

Select [OK] to display the SQL QUERY COLUMNS window. Add **Identification Number**, **DIVISION**, **Education level**, and **Salary** to the Selected Columns list.

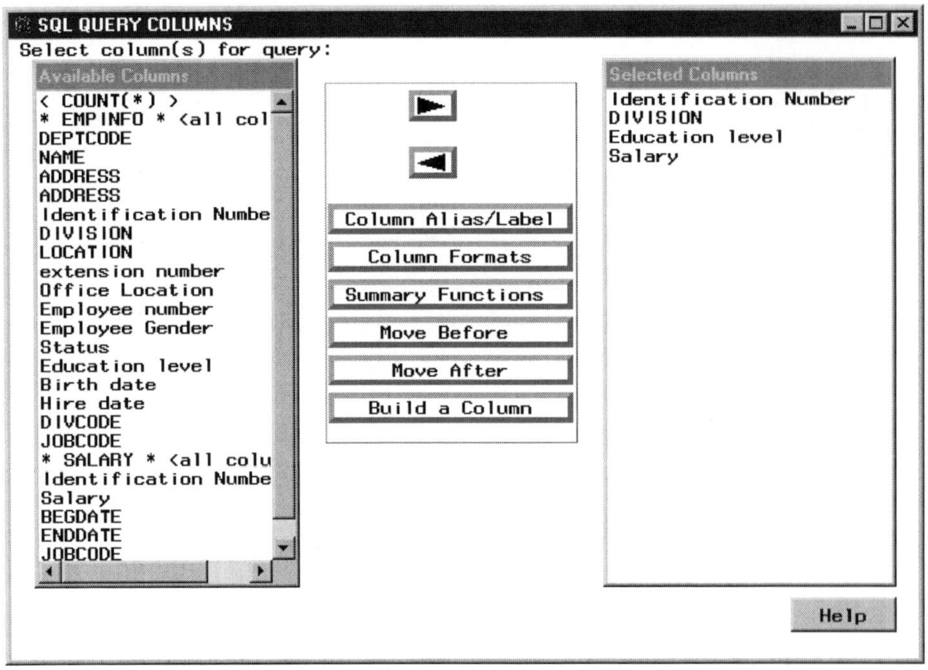

Select **View ▶ Join Type**. Select **Matched Join** from the Join Types window to create an inner join. Select [OK].

Select **Identification Number** from both lists in the Columns for Setting Join Criteria window.

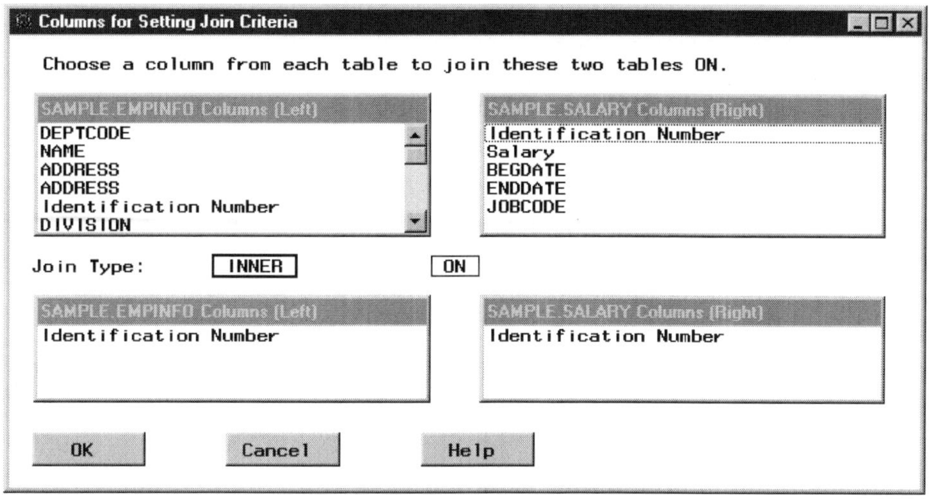

Select [OK].

Producing Output with the REPORT Procedure

Select **Tools ► Run Query ► Design a Report ► Begin with default report**. The output from your query appears in a PROC REPORT window.

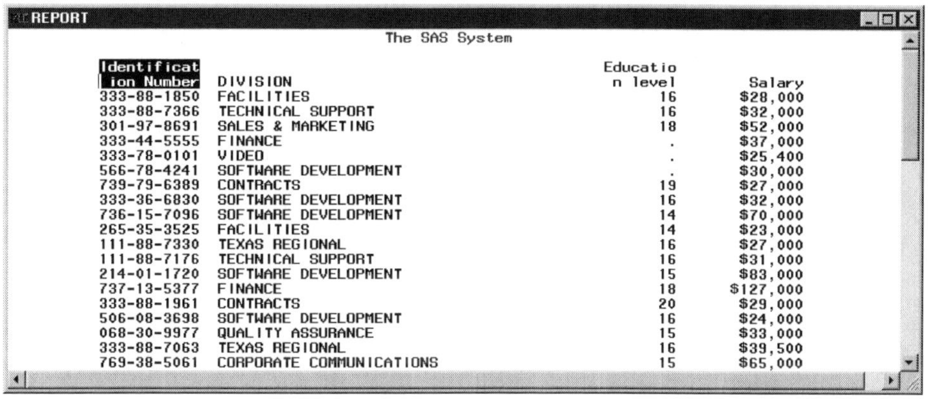

Modifying the Format of Your Report

You can now modify your report.

Set Report Options

In the REPORT window, select **Tools ► Options ► Report**.

In the ROPTIONS window, type **80** in the Linesize field to set the width of the output. Type **60** in the Pagesize field. Select the **HEADLINE** and **HEADSKIP** check boxes.

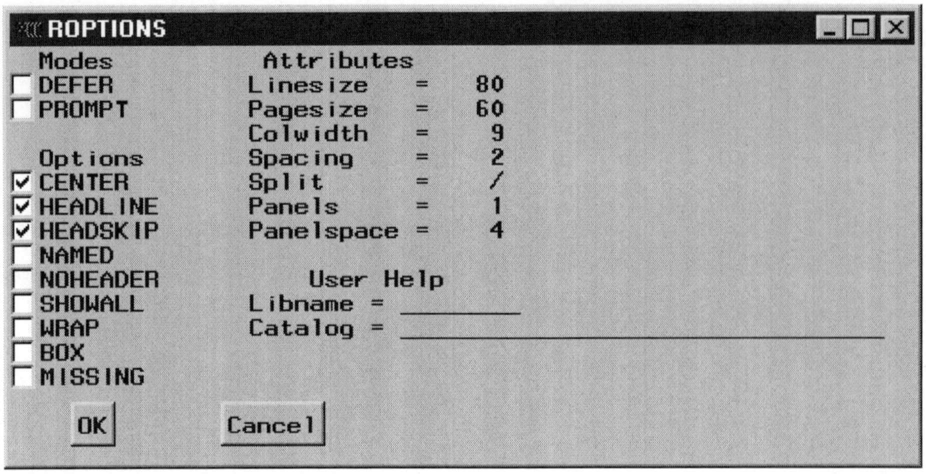

Select OK.

Define Selected Item

Select the **`Identification Number`** heading. Select **Edit ▶ Define**.

Select **`NOPRINT`** in the DEFINITION window to prevent the identification number from being displayed.

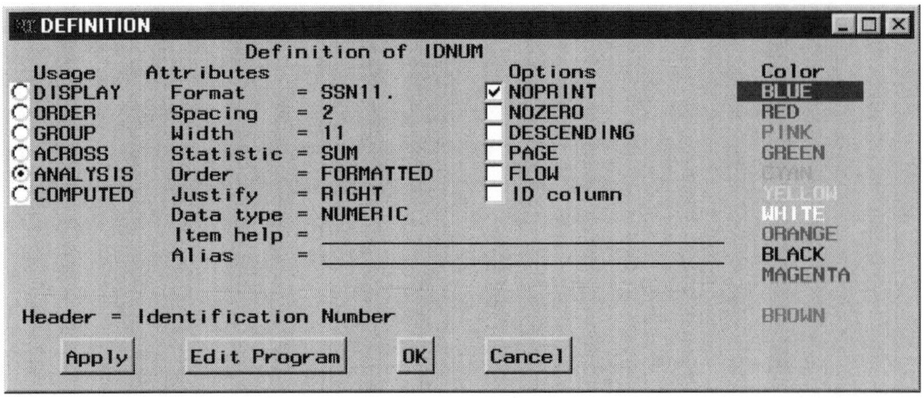

Select OK.

Move Selected Item

In the REPORT window, select the **`Education level`** heading. Select **Edit ▶ Move ▶ Left of the Next Selected Item**.

Select the **`DIVISION`** heading in the REPORT window. Education Level appears as the first column in the window.

Select the **`Education level`** heading in the REPORT window. Select **Edit ▶ Define**.

In the DEFINITION window, select **`ORDER`**. Type **`2.`** in the Format field. Type **`15`** in the Width field. Type **`CENTER`** in the Justify field.

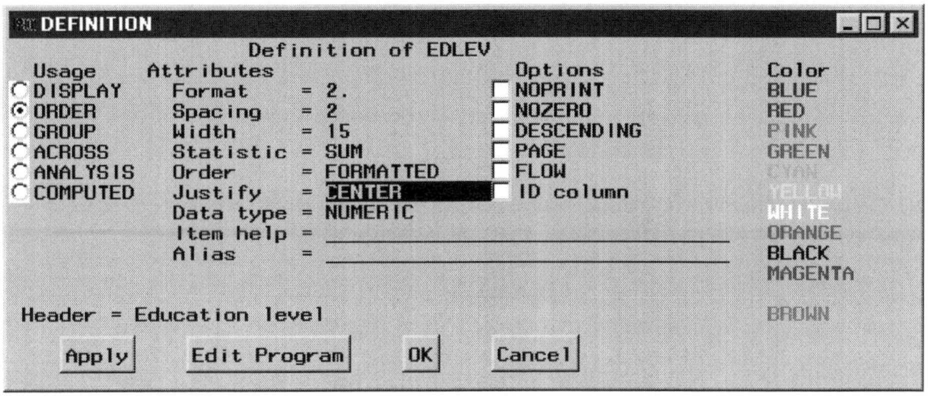

Select [OK].

Select the **Salary** heading in the REPORT window. Select **Edit ▶ Move ▶ Left of the Next Selected Item**.

Select the **Division** heading. Salary will appear as the second column in the window.

Select the **Salary** heading. Select **Edit ▶ Define**.

In the DEFINITION window, type **DOLLAR8.** in the Format field. Type **8** in the Width field.

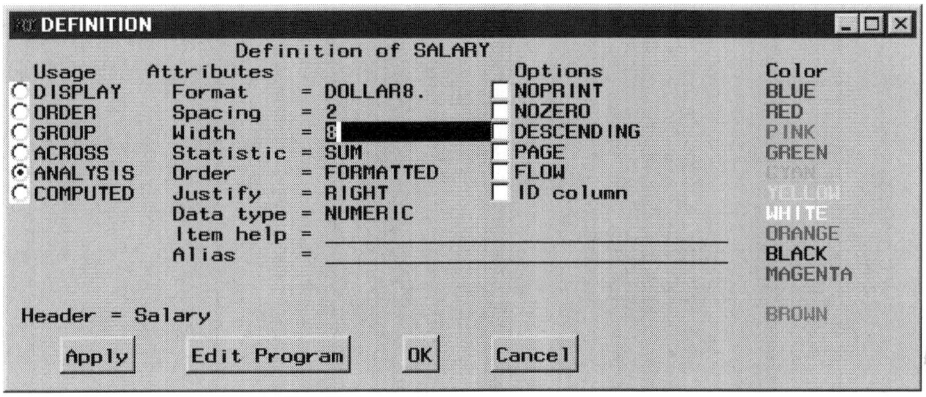

Select [OK].

Select the **DIVISION** heading in the REPORT window. Select **Edit ▶ Define**.

Type **$30.** in the Format field of the DEFINITION window. Type **30** in the Width field.

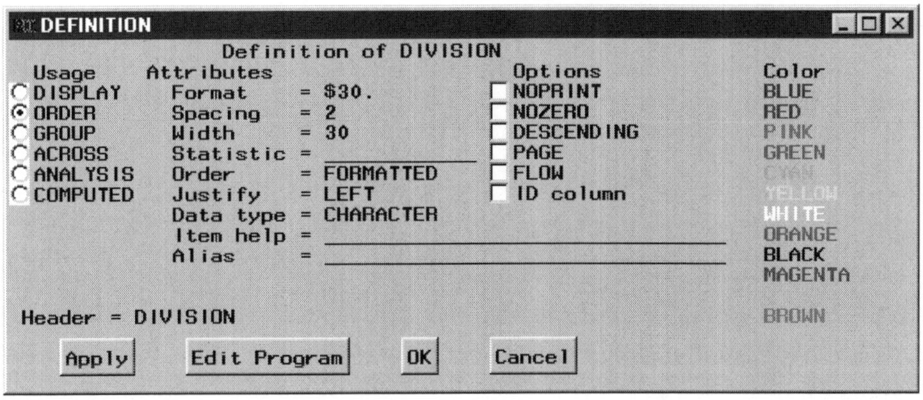

Select [OK].

The Formatted Report

Your completed report compares the salaries of employees from different divisions who have the same education level.

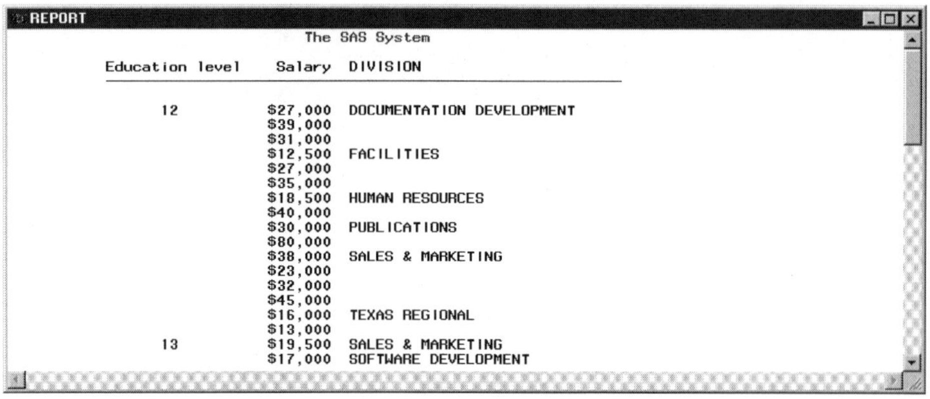
```
REPORT
                          The SAS System

   Education level     Salary  DIVISION
   --------------------------------------------------------
         12           $27,000  DOCUMENTATION DEVELOPMENT
                      $39,000
                      $31,000
                      $12,500  FACILITIES
                      $27,000
                      $35,000
                      $18,500  HUMAN RESOURCES
                      $40,000
                      $30,000  PUBLICATIONS
                      $80,000
                      $38,000  SALES & MARKETING
                      $23,000
                      $32,000
                      $45,000
                      $16,000  TEXAS REGIONAL
                      $13,000
         13           $19,500  SALES & MARKETING
                      $17,000  SOFTWARE DEVELOPMENT
```

Viewing the Report Statements

You can view your report statements in the SOURCE window by selecting **Tools ▶ REPORT Statements**.

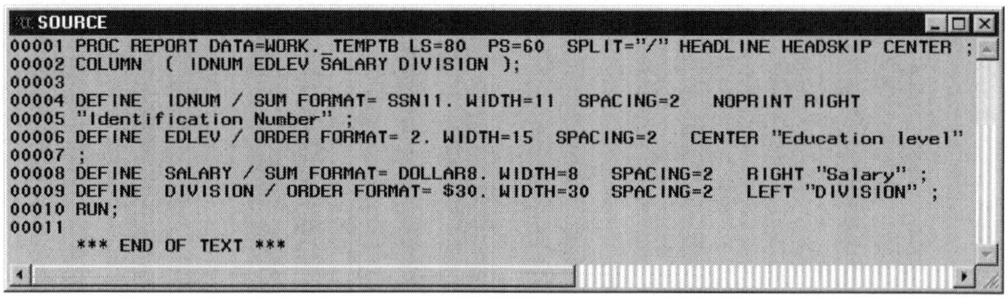
```
SOURCE
PROC REPORT DATA=WORK._TEMPTB LS=80  PS=60  SPLIT="/" HEADLINE HEADSKIP CENTER ;
COLUMN  ( IDNUM EDLEV SALARY DIVISION );

DEFINE  IDNUM / SUM FORMAT= SSN11. WIDTH=11  SPACING=2   NOPRINT RIGHT
"Identification Number" ;
DEFINE  EDLEV / ORDER FORMAT= 2. WIDTH=15  SPACING=2   CENTER "Education level"
;
DEFINE  SALARY / SUM FORMAT= DOLLAR8. WIDTH=8   SPACING=2   RIGHT "Salary" ;
DEFINE  DIVISION / ORDER FORMAT= $30. WIDTH=30  SPACING=2   LEFT "DIVISION" ;
RUN;

    *** END OF TEXT ***
```

Select **File ▶ Close** to close the SOURCE window and return to the REPORT window.

Saving Your Report

You can save your customized report to a catalog entry for use with later queries by selecting **File ▶ Save Report** to display the SAVE DEFINITION window. Type **`SAMPLE`** in the Libname field. Type **`SQL`** in the Catalog field. Type **`SALARY`** in the Report name field. Type **`Salaries and Divisions`** in the Description field.

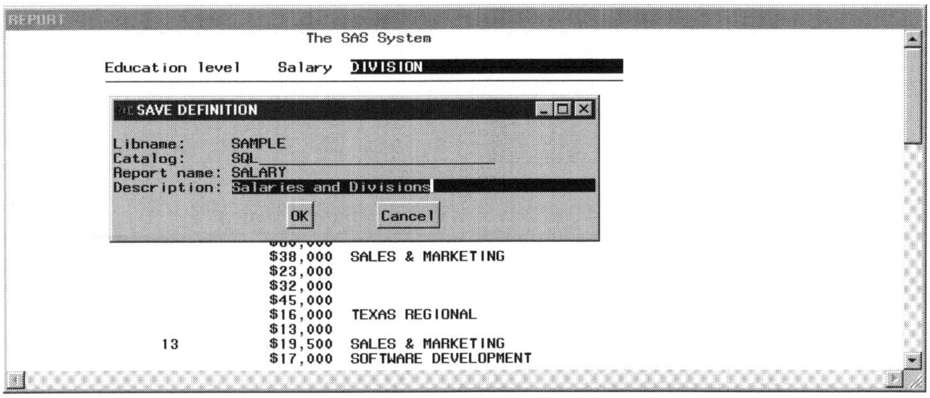

Select OK. A dialog box appears that notifies you of the creation of a new catalog. Select OK.

Select **File ▶ Close** to exit the REPORT window. Select OK in the dialog box that appears.

You can also save your report definition in the SQL Query Window when you save the query.

Use Definition from Last Report

You can use your customized report definition. In the SQL QUERY COLUMNS window, select **Tools ▶ Run Query ▶ Design a Report ▶ Use definition from last Report**.

The results of the query are presented using your predefined report.

Select **File ▶ Close** to exit the REPORT window. Select OK in the dialog box that appears.

Creating Summary Reports

You can use the SQL Query window in conjunction with the REPORT Procedure to create a summary report with totals.

Using a Saved Report Definition

For this example you will modify the report that you created in the previous example to display the total salaries for each division. In the SQL QUERY COLUMNS window, select **Tools ▶ Run Query ▶ Design a Report ▶ Name a predefined report**. When the dialog box appears, select **SAMPLE** from the Libraries list. The libraries and catalogs that are listed in your display might differ from the ones in the example.

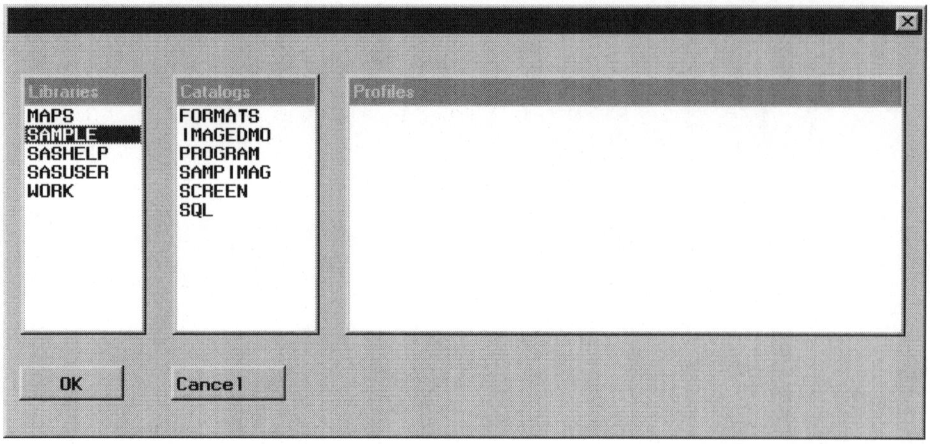

Select **`SQL`** from the Catalogs list. Select the **`SALARY`** report definition. Select [OK].

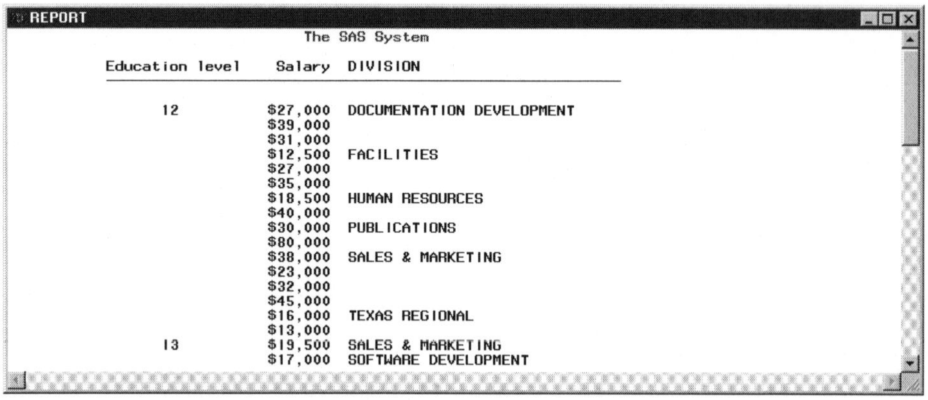

Deleting a Heading

You do not need to display education level for this report. In the REPORT window, select the **`Education level`** heading. Select **Edit ▶ Delete** to delete the Education Level column from the report. You are not deleting EDUCATION LEVEL from the query.

Summarizing Information

Select the **`DIVISION`** heading. Select **Edit ▶ Summarize Information ▶ After Item** to display the BREAK window. Select the **`Double overline summary`** check box to print a double line over the summary total. Select the **`Skip line after break`** and **`Summarize analysis columns`** check boxes.

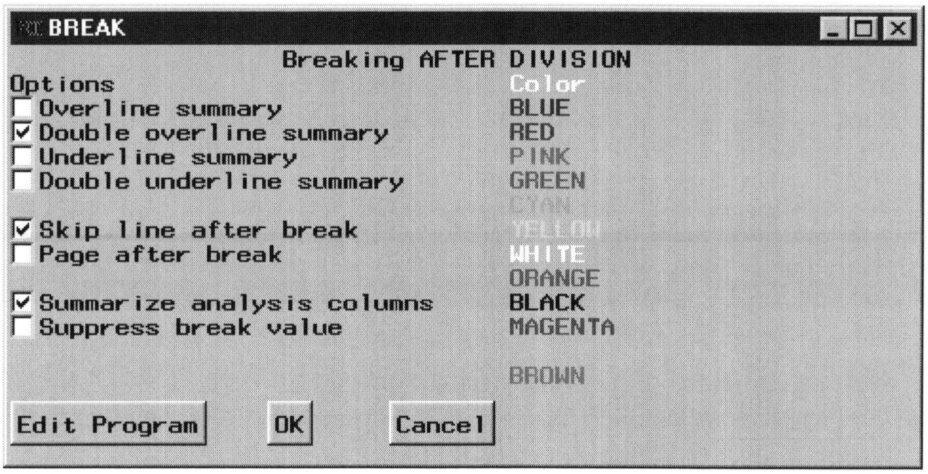

Select [OK] to return to the REPORT window and display the total salaries for each division.

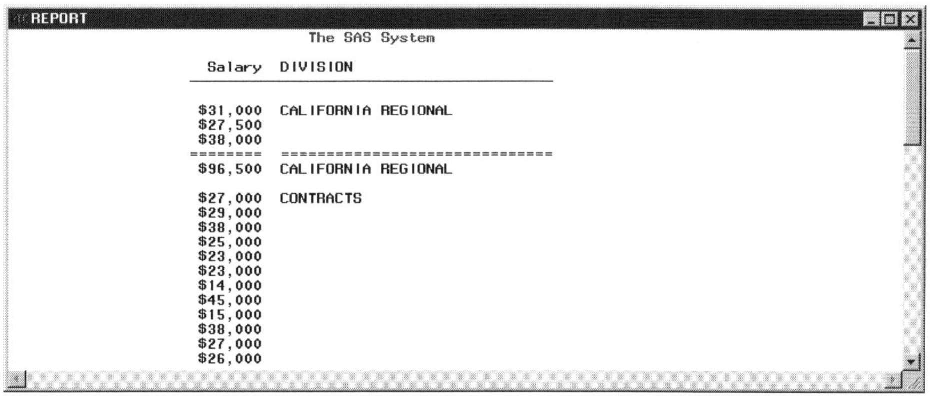

Select **File ▶ Close**.

Select [OK] in the dialog box that appears. The SQL QUERY COLUMNS window reappears.

Select **Tools ▶ Reset** to reset the query and return to the SQL QUERY TABLES window.

Counting and Grouping Data Automatically

You can count and report the total number of rows that have the same value for one or more columns. You can use the automatic group-by feature to group the values according to their columns.

The following query displays the number of employees in each division.

In the SQL QUERY TABLES window, select **`SAMPLE.EMPINFO`** from the Available Tables list and add it to the Selected Tables list. Select [OK].

In the SQL QUERY COLUMNS window, select **`DIVISION`** and **`< COUNT(*) >`** from the Available Columns list and add them to the Selected Columns list.

Count

Select **COUNT(*)** from the Selected Columns List. Select [Move After] to move the column. Reselect **COUNT(*)**. Select [Column Alias/Label]. Type **Count of Employees for Each Division** in the Label field of the Column Alias and Label window.

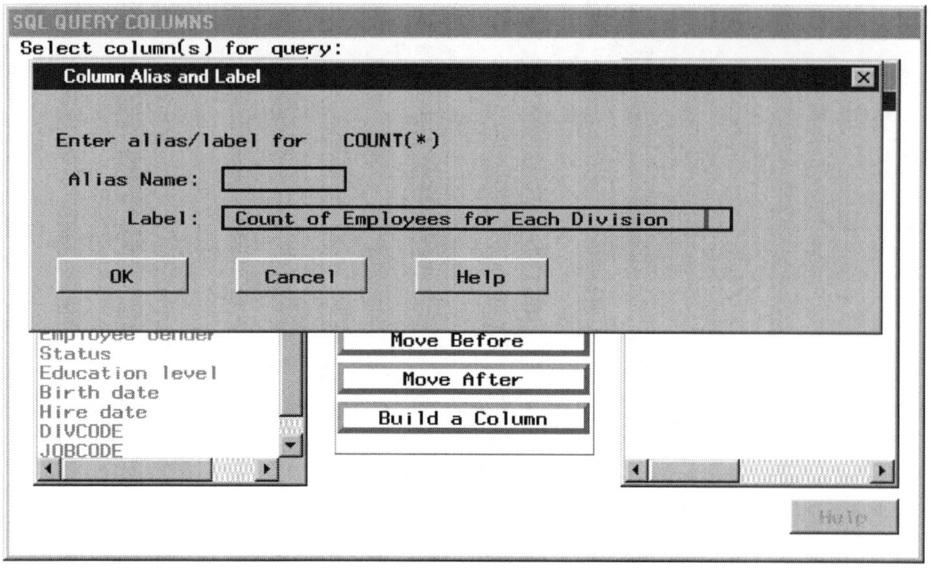

Select [OK].

Grouping Columns Automatically

Select **Tools ▸ Run Query ▸ Run Immediate**. A dialog box appears.

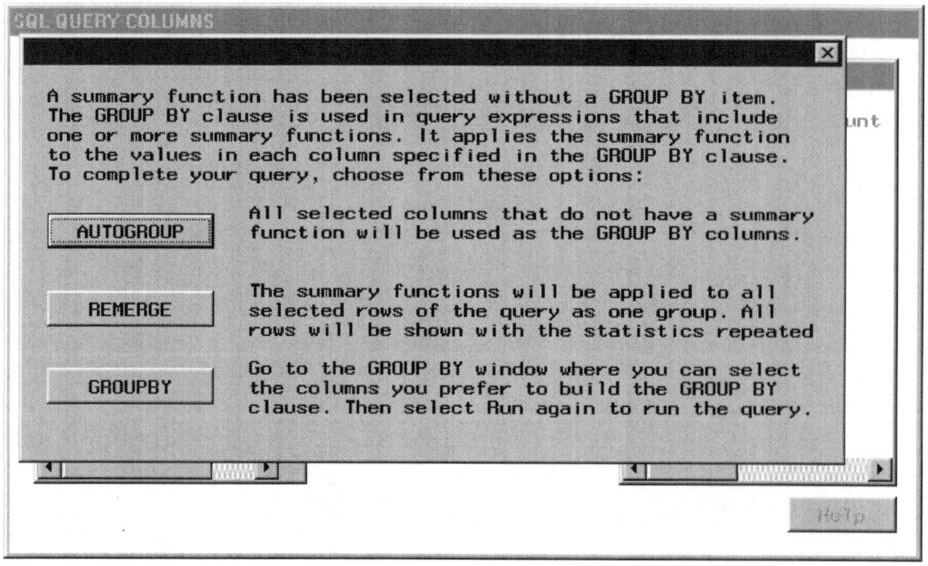

Select [AUTOGROUP] to automatically select the correct columns. Selected columns that do not have summary functions applied to them will be the group or groups that the summary functions are computed for.

A second dialog box appears.

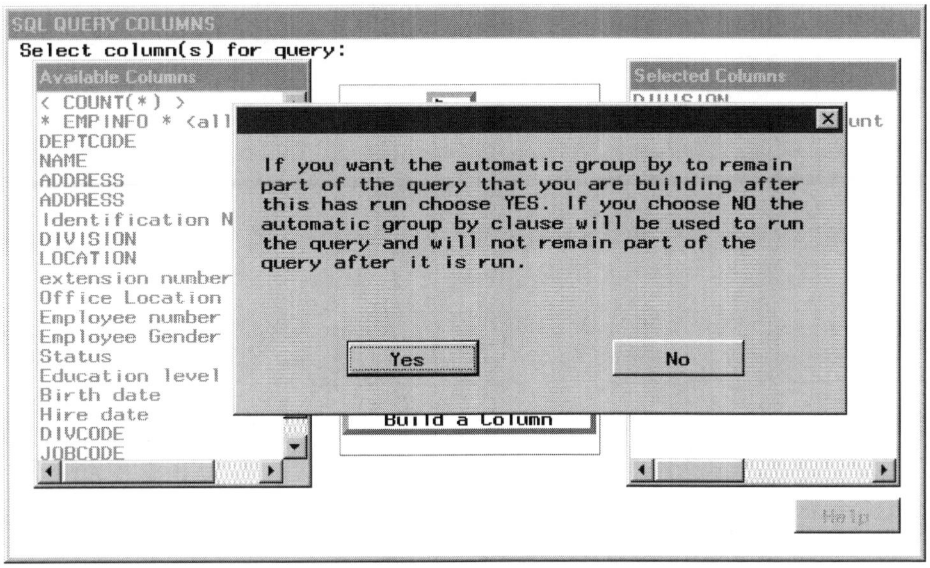

Select [No]. The automatic Group By clause will be part of the query syntax while the query runs, but it will not be retained. You can select or remove columns after the query is executed and use [AUTOGROUP] to automatically select the columns again.

The count of employees for each division is displayed in the Output window.

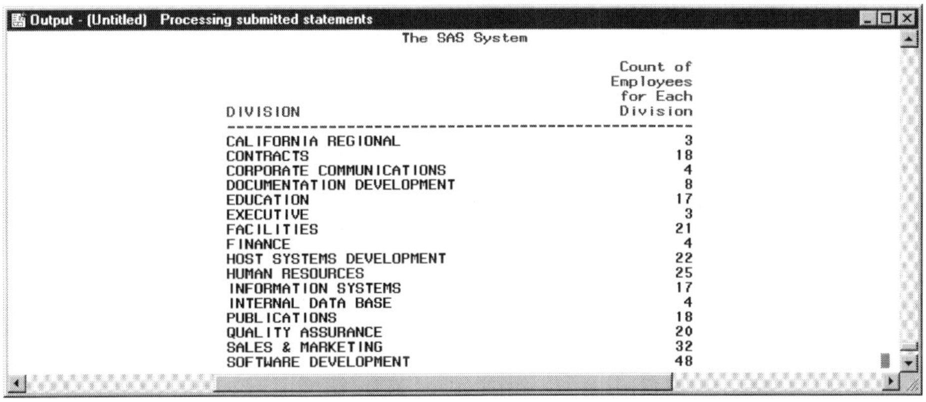

In the SQL QUERY COLUMNS window, select **Tools ▸ Reset** to reset your query. Select [OK] from the dialog box that appears.

Automatic Group By with More Than One Table

The next query joins two tables to display the number of employees for each job title. The JOBCODES table contains the job title for each job code.

Select **SAMPLE.JOBCODES** and **SAMPLE.EMPINFO** from the Available Tables list and add them to the Selected Tables list.

Select [OK].

In the SQL QUERY COLUMNS window, select **TITLE** and **< COUNT(*) >** from the Available Columns list and add them to the Selected Columns list.

Select **View ▸ Where Conditions for Subset**.

In the WHERE EXPRESSION window, select **EMPINFO.JOBCODE** from the Available Columns list. Select **EQ** from the list of comparison operators.

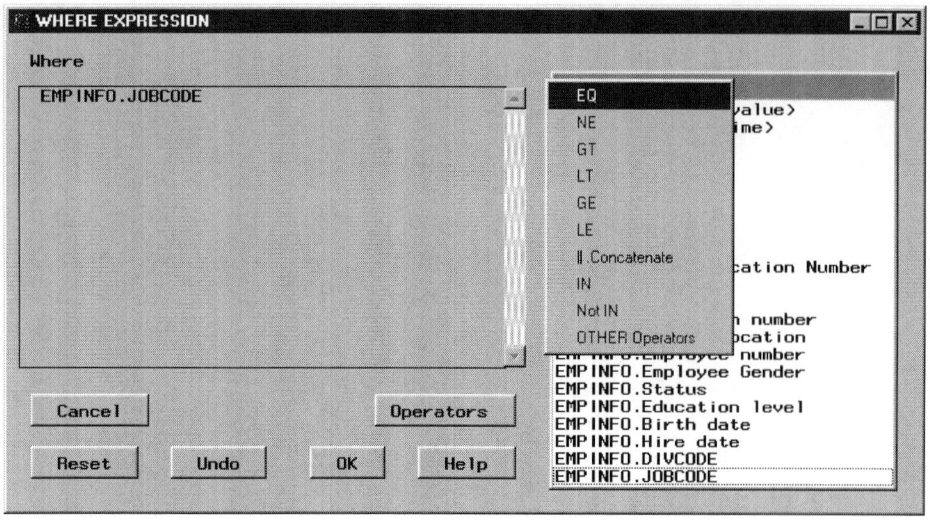

Select **JOBCODES.JOBCODE** from the Available Columns list.

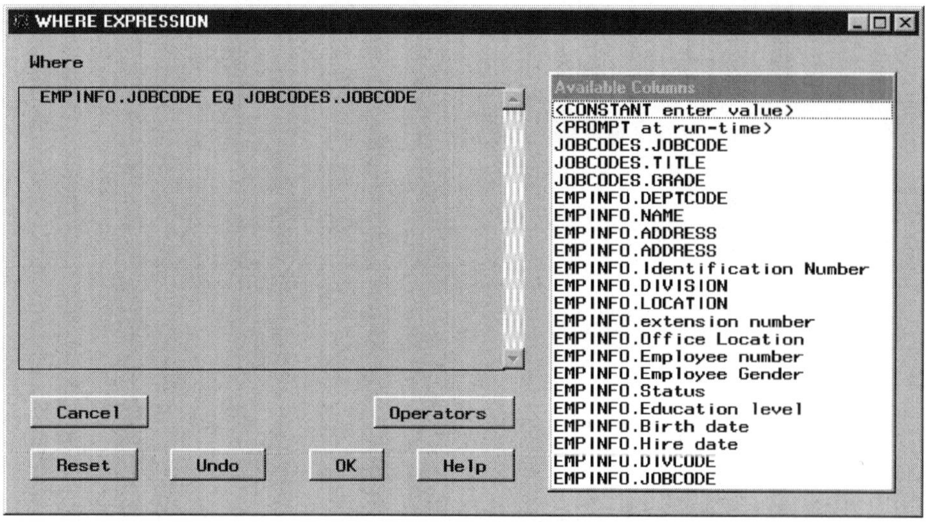

Select OK to return to the SQL QUERY COLUMNS window.

Select **COUNT(*)** from the Selected Columns List. Select Move After to move the column. Reselect **COUNT(*)**. Select Column Alias/Label. Type **Count of Employees for Each Title** in the Label field of the Column Alias and Label window.

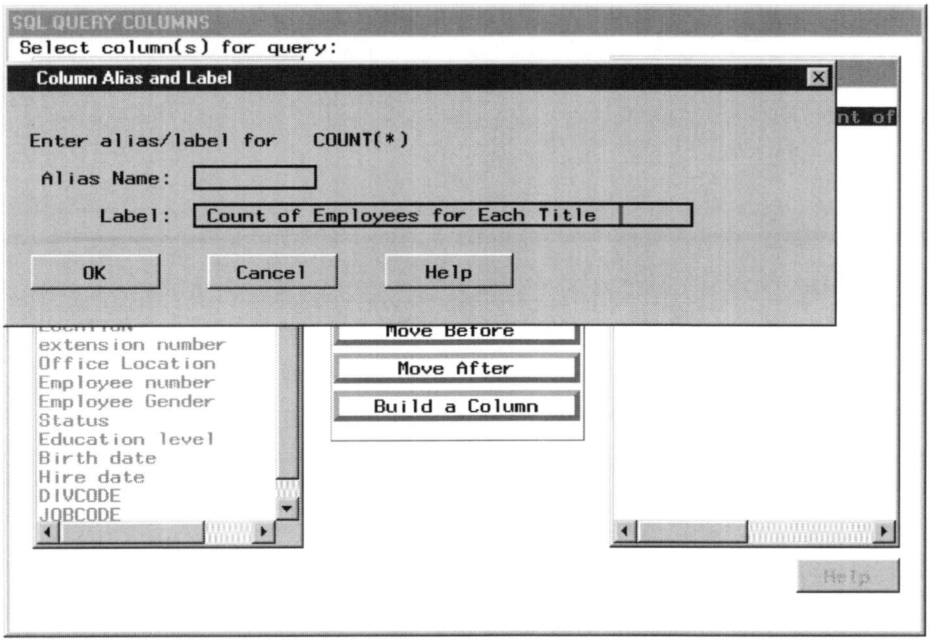

Select [OK].

Retaining an Automatic Group By as Part of a Query

Select **Tools ► Run Query ► Run Immediate**. A dialog box appears. Select [AUTOGROUP] in the dialog box to use JOBCODES.TITLE as the Group By column. A second dialog box appears. Select [Yes] in the second dialog box to retain the Group By column as part of the query.

The Output window displays the number of employees for each job title.

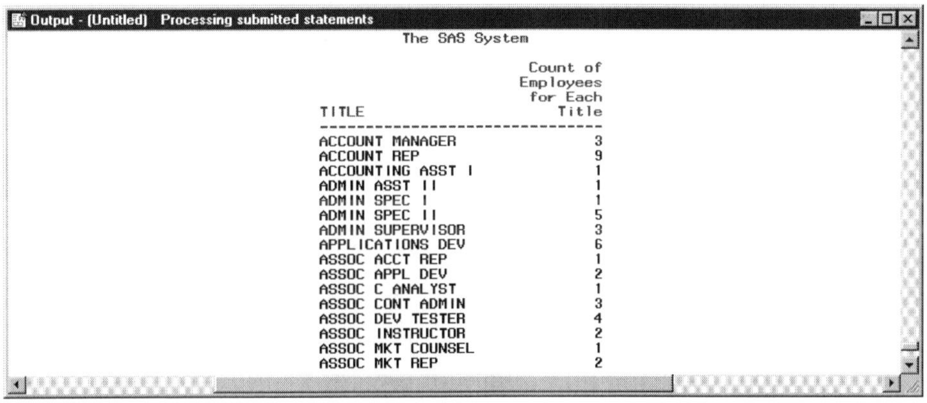

TITLE	Count of Employees for Each Title
ACCOUNT MANAGER	3
ACCOUNT REP	9
ACCOUNTING ASST I	1
ADMIN ASST II	1
ADMIN SPEC I	1
ADMIN SPEC II	5
ADMIN SUPERVISOR	3
APPLICATIONS DEV	6
ASSOC ACCT REP	1
ASSOC APPL DEV	2
ASSOC C ANALYST	1
ASSOC CONT ADMIN	3
ASSOC DEV TESTER	4
ASSOC INSTRUCTOR	2
ASSOC MKT COUNSEL	1
ASSOC MKT REP	2

In the SQL QUERY COLUMNS window, select **Tools ► Show Query**.

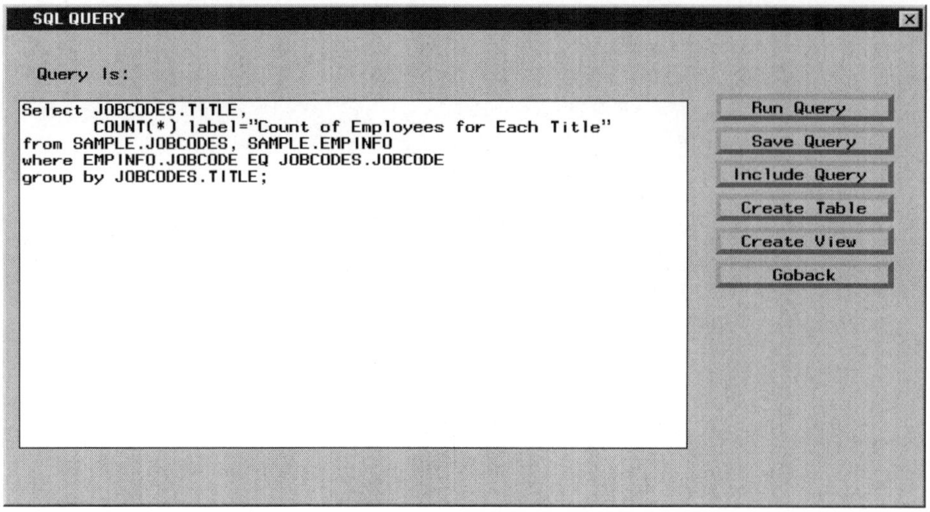

The automatic Group By will be retained as part of the query syntax when the query is run again, saved, or used to create a table or view. Select [Goback] to return to the SQL QUERY COLUMNS window.

In the SQL QUERY COLUMNS window, select **File ▶ Save Query ▶ Save as QUERY to Include later**.

In the Entry Name field, type **`COUNTS`** as the name of the query. In the description field, type **`Count of EMPNO by TITLE`**. Select [OK] to save the query and return to the SQL QUERY COLUMNS window.

Select **View ▶ Tables** to return to the SQL QUERY TABLES window. Remove **`SALARY.JOBCODES`** from the Selected Tables list. Select [OK] in the dialog box that appears.

Summarizing Groups of Data

Summary functions produce a statistical summary of a table or groups of data. The following example displays the minimum, average, and maximum level of employee education within each division. Use the Group By clause and a summary function to summarize information about a group of data. If you omit a Group By, then one summary value is produced for the entire table.

Summary Functions

The Selected Tables list in the SQL QUERY TABLES window contains **`SAMPLE.EMPINFO`** from the previous example. Select [OK].

In the SQL QUERY COLUMNS window, remove **`COUNT(*)`** from the Selected Columns list. Select **`DIVISION`** and **`Education level`** from the Available Columns list and add them to the Selected Columns list.

Select **`Education level`** a second time from the Available Columns List and add it to the Selected Columns list.

Select **`Education level`** a third time from the Available Columns list and add it to the Selected Columns list.

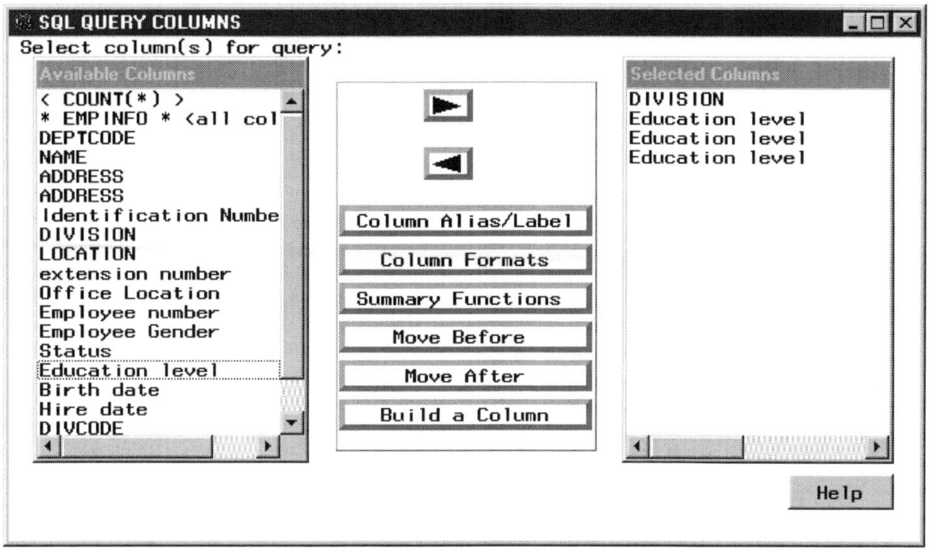

Select the first **Education level** from the Selected Columns list. Select [Summary Functions].

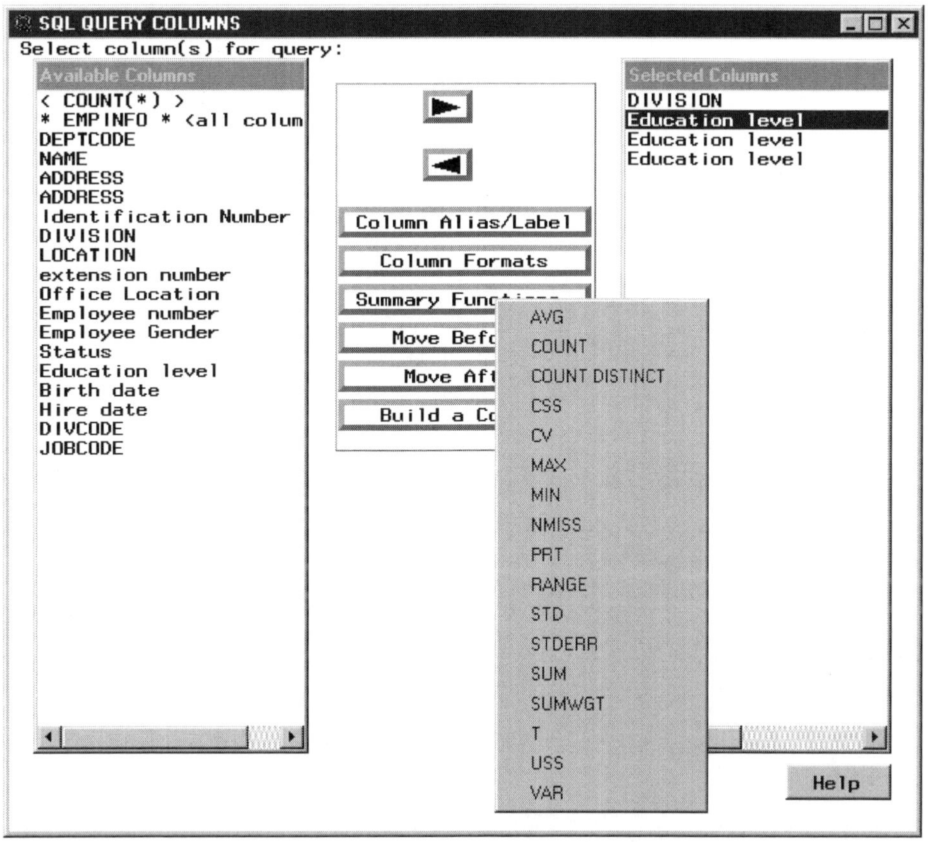

Select **MIN** from the list of summary functions. A summary function is applied to the selected column and a default unique column alias is automatically generated. The summary function and the selected column name are automatically set as the label. You can use this default label in the report, or you can set a new alias or label.

Select the second **Education level** from the Selected Columns list. Select [Summary Functions]. Select **AVG** from the list of summary functions.

Select the third **Education level** from the Selected Columns list. Select [Summary Functions]. Select **MAX** from the list of summary functions.

Select the first **Education level** from the Selected Columns list. Select [Column Alias/Label]. Type **Minimum Years of Education** in the Label field of the Column Alias and Label window.

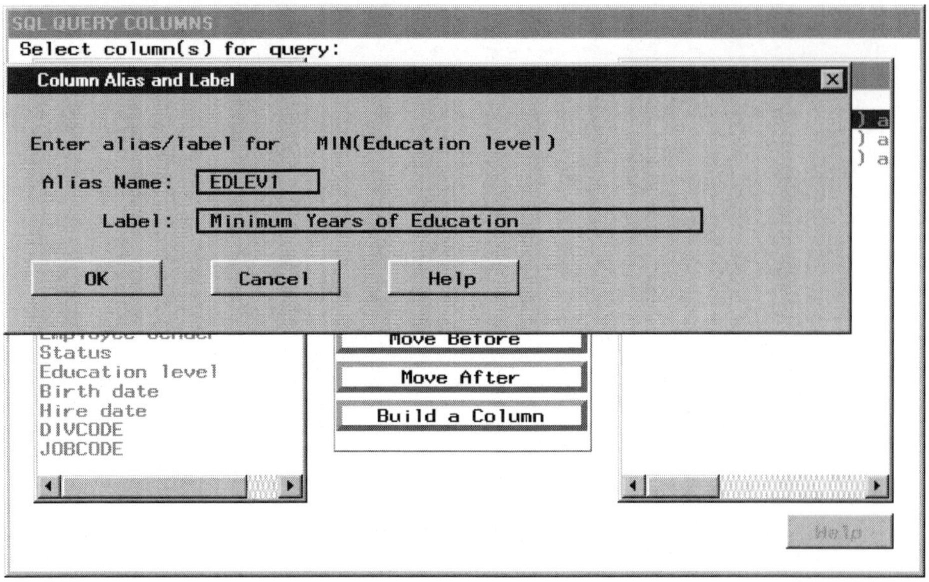

Select [OK].

Select the second **Education level** from the Selected Columns list. Select [Column Alias/Label]. Type **Average Years of Education** in the Label field of the Column Alias and Label window.

Select [OK].

Select the third **Education level** from the Selected Columns list. Select [Column Alias/Label]. Type **Maximum Years of Education** in the Label field of the Column Alias and Label window.

Select [OK].

Select the second **Education level** from the Selected Columns list. Select [Column Formats].

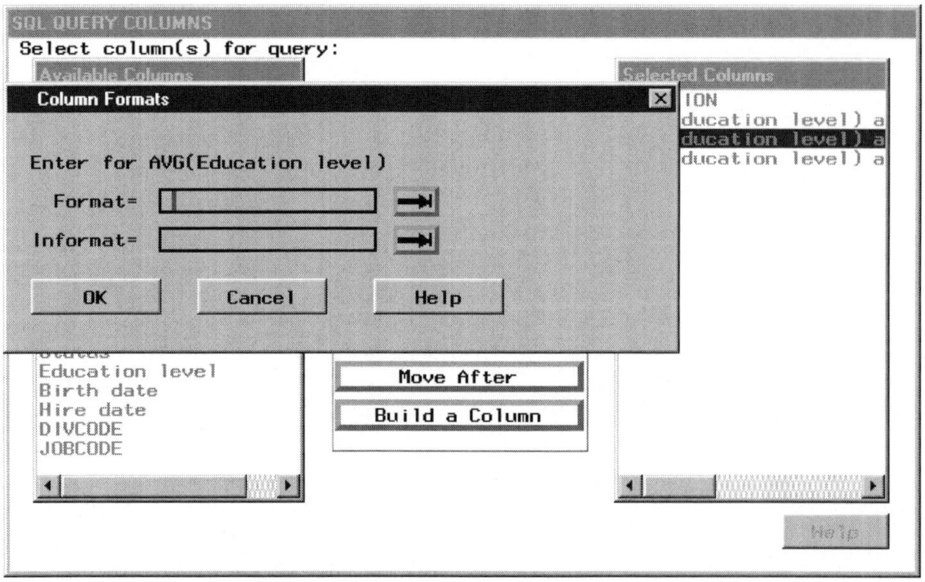

Type **comma4.0** in the Format field. Select [OK].
Select **Tools ► Run Query ► Run Immediate**. A dialog box appears.

Group By Columns

Select [GROUPBY] to display the GROUP BY COLUMNS window.

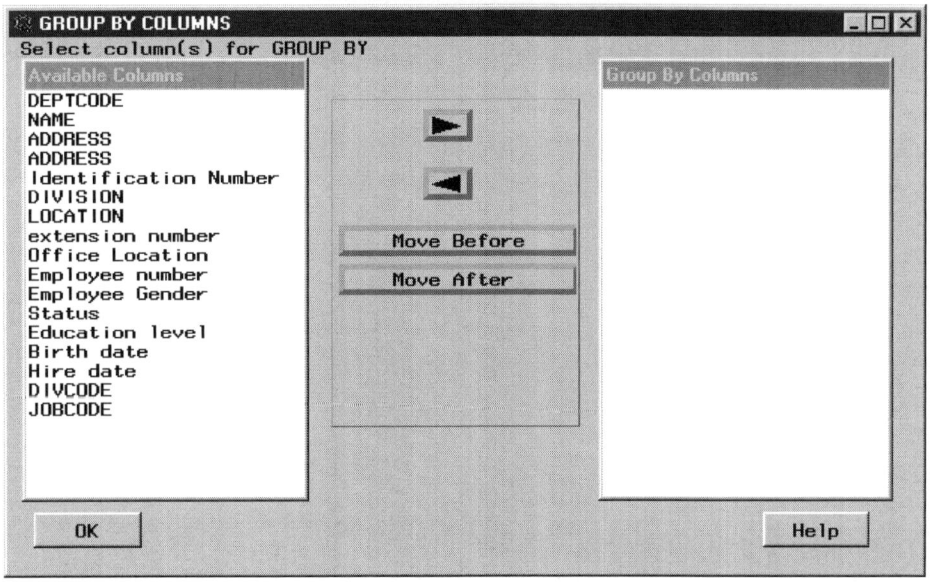

Select **DIVISION** from the Available Columns list and add it to the Group By Columns list. Select [OK].

The minimum, average, and maximum education levels of the employees for each division are displayed in the Output window.

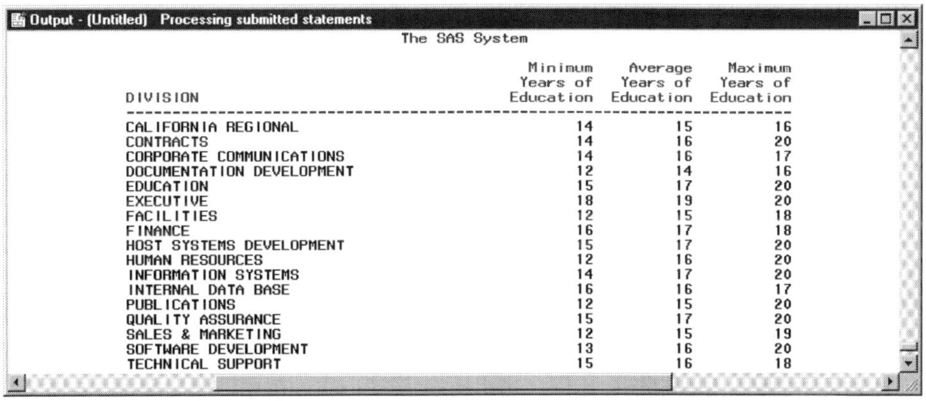
Output - (Untitled) Processing submitted statements

The SAS System

DIVISION	Minimum Years of Education	Average Years of Education	Maximum Years of Education
CALIFORNIA REGIONAL	14	15	16
CONTRACTS	14	16	20
CORPORATE COMMUNICATIONS	14	16	17
DOCUMENTATION DEVELOPMENT	12	14	16
EDUCATION	15	17	20
EXECUTIVE	18	19	20
FACILITIES	12	15	18
FINANCE	16	17	18
HOST SYSTEMS DEVELOPMENT	15	17	20
HUMAN RESOURCES	12	16	20
INFORMATION SYSTEMS	14	17	20
INTERNAL DATA BASE	16	16	17
PUBLICATIONS	12	15	20
QUALITY ASSURANCE	15	17	20
SALES & MARKETING	12	15	19
SOFTWARE DEVELOPMENT	13	16	20
TECHNICAL SUPPORT	15	16	18

In the SQL QUERY COLUMNS window, select **Tools ► Reset** to reset your query and return to the SQL QUERY TABLES window. Select [OK] from the dialog box that appears.

Removing Duplicate Rows

You can remove duplicate rows from your query output. To display each distinct division and location, select **SAMPLE.EMPINFO** and add it to the Selected Tables list. Select [OK].

In the SQL QUERY COLUMNS window, select **DIVISION** and **LOCATION** and add them to the Selected Columns list.

Select **View ▶ Distinct**.

Select **Tools ▶ Run Query ▶ Run Immediate**. Lines in the Output window that contain the same division and location are not repeated.

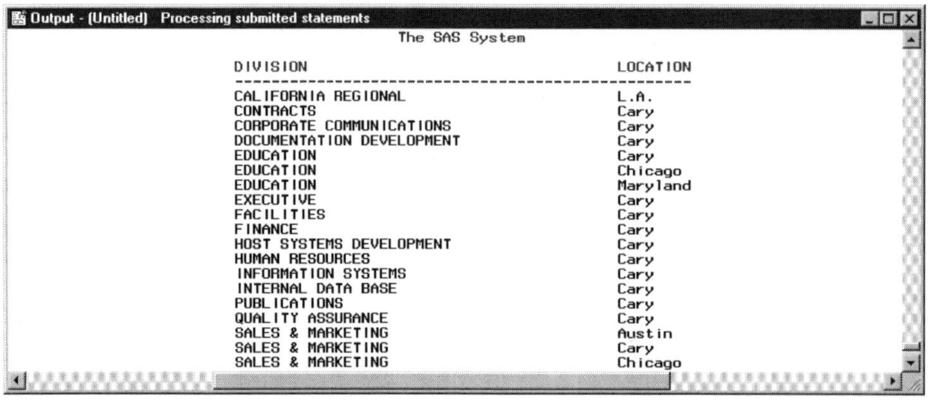

DIVISION	LOCATION
CALIFORNIA REGIONAL	L.A.
CONTRACTS	Cary
CORPORATE COMMUNICATIONS	Cary
DOCUMENTATION DEVELOPMENT	Cary
EDUCATION	Cary
EDUCATION	Chicago
EDUCATION	Maryland
EXECUTIVE	Cary
FACILITIES	Cary
FINANCE	Cary
HOST SYSTEMS DEVELOPMENT	Cary
HUMAN RESOURCES	Cary
INFORMATION SYSTEMS	Cary
INTERNAL DATA BASE	Cary
PUBLICATIONS	Cary
QUALITY ASSURANCE	Cary
SALES & MARKETING	Austin
SALES & MARKETING	Cary
SALES & MARKETING	Chicago

In the SQL QUERY COLUMNS window, select **Tools ▶ Reset** to reset your query and return to the SQL QUERY TABLES window. Select [OK] from the dialog box that appears.

Subsetting Groups of Data with the HAVING Condition

The HAVING condition specifies the condition or conditions that each group must satisfy in order to be included in the query output. You can use a HAVING condition to subset grouped data by using HAVING in the same query with a GROUPBY and a summary function.

Which divisions in the previous example have a minimum employee education level that is greater than 15 years? To find out, select **SAMPLE.EMPINFO** and add it to the Selected Tables list. Select [OK].

In the SQL QUERY COLUMNS window, select **DIVISION** and add it to the Selected Columns list. Remove duplicate values by selecting **View ▶ Distinct**.

HAVING EXPRESSION Window

To create a condition that each output group must satisfy, select **View ▶ Having Condition for Group** to display the HAVING EXPRESSION window.

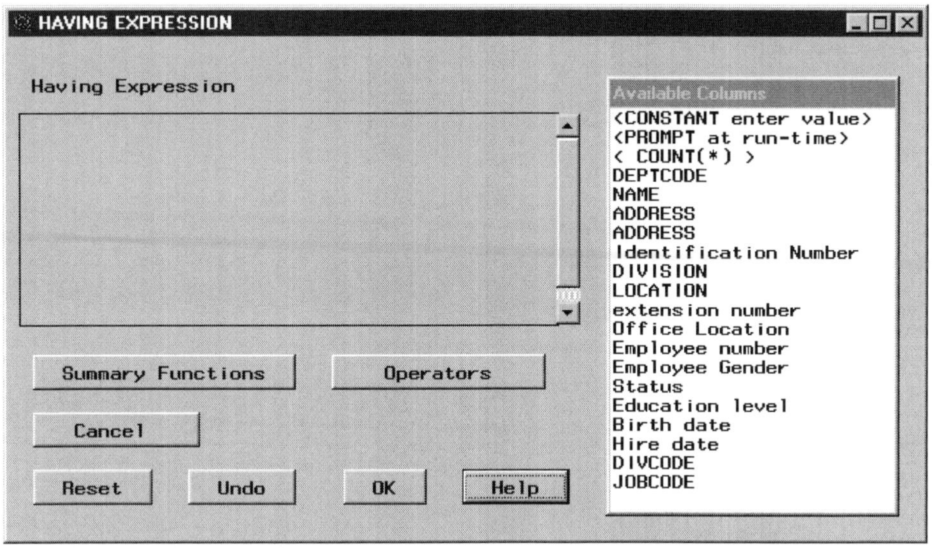

Select [Summary Functions]. Select **`MIN`** from the list of summary functions.

Select **`Education level`** from the Available Columns list.

Select **`GT`** from the list of operators that appears.

Select **`<CONSTANT enter value>`** from the Available Columns list. The Numeric Values dialog box appears.

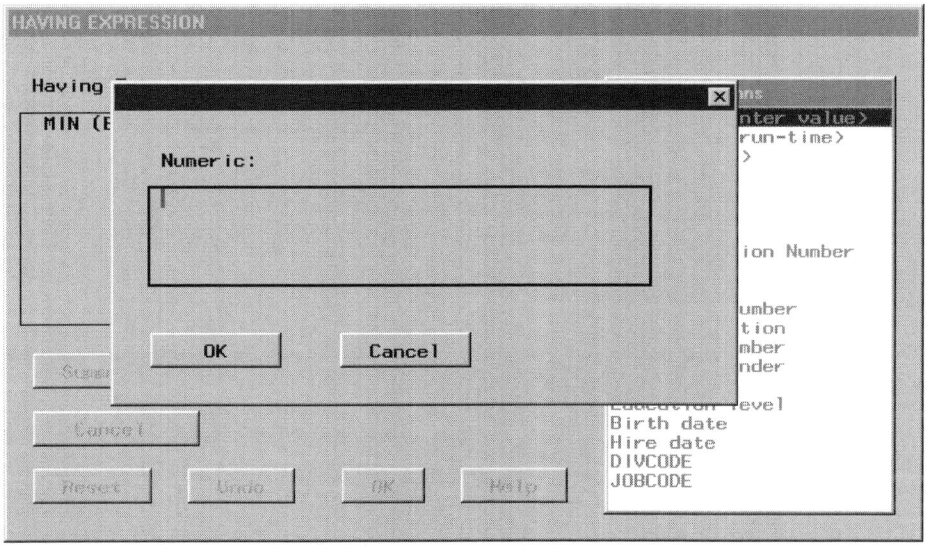

Type **`15`** in the Numeric field and select [OK].

In the HAVING EXPRESSION window, select [OK] to return to the SQL QUERY COLUMNS window.

Viewing the Results of the HAVING Condition

Select **View ▶ Group(s) for Summary Functions** to display the GROUP BY COLUMNS window.

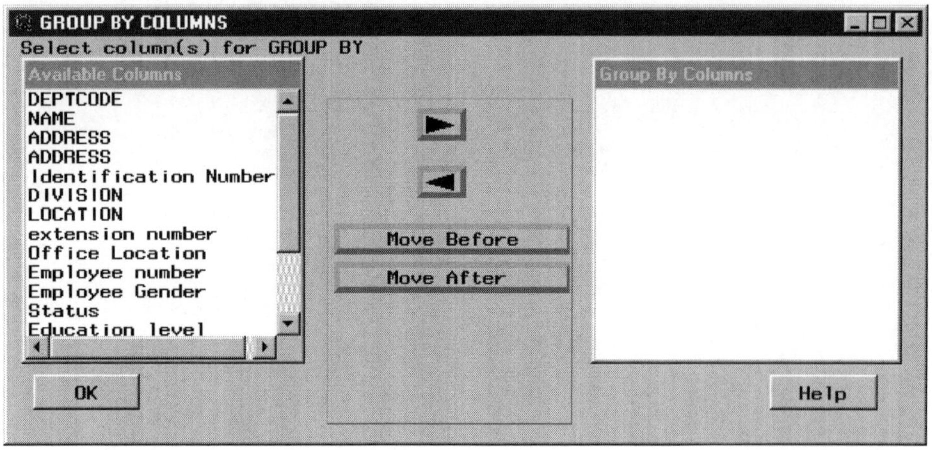

Select **DIVISION** from the Available Columns list and add it to the Group By Columns list.

Select OK.

Select **Tools ▶ Run Query ▶ Run Immediate** to display the divisions whose minimum employee education level is greater than 15.

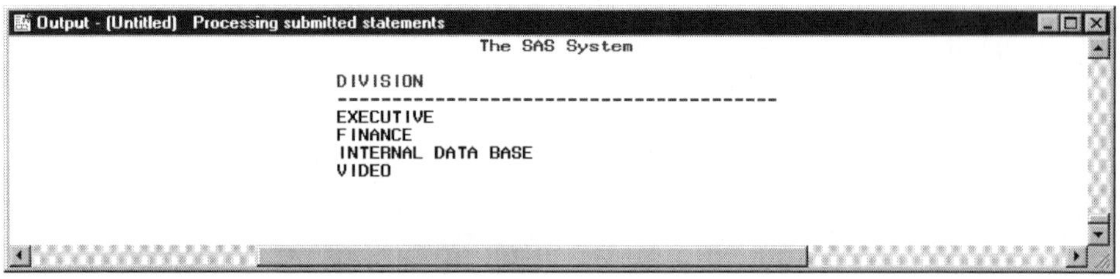

In the SQL QUERY COLUMNS window, select **Tools ▶ Reset** to reset the query and return to the SQL QUERY TABLES window. Select OK from the dialog box that appears.

Using the Automatic Lookup Feature

You can implement automatic lookup for any column in a table that can be accessed from the SQL Query window. Automatic lookup causes an action, that varies according to the lookup strategy, to automatically occur when that column and an operator are selected from the WHERE EXPRESSION window.

In this example, you implement automatic lookup by creating a SAS data set called a lookup table. You then insert a set of values into the lookup table for each column for which you want a Lookup Values window to be displayed.

Lookup Strategies

You can specify any one of five lookup strategies for each column:

V (Value)
: automatically retrieves the distinct values of the column that has been specified in the lookup table. The distinct values appear in a Lookup Values window in the WHERE EXPRESSION window when you have selected both the specified column

from the Available Columns window and an operator from the menu that subsequently appears. When you select one or more values, these values are inserted into the WHERE expression. The EQ operator is converted to the IN operator to allow multiple selections.

T (Table)
: reads a table and displays the values of all the columns in the Lookup Values window. The first column in the table must contain the values that are needed in the WHERE expression. You can use other columns to provide descriptive information.

  If the first column contains a small number of distinct rows in comparison to the number of rows in the table, then the distinct values and their descriptions can be stored in a separate table. This table can be used to display automatic lookup values for the subset conditions.

L (List)
: enables you to select specific columns from a table for display in the Lookup Values window. The first column that you specify must contain the values that are needed for the WHERE expression. You can use other columns to provide descriptive data values.

F (Format)
: displays column data values and their corresponding formatted values that have been created with the FORMAT procedure.

P (Program)
: invokes a user-written SAS/AF program. A list that contains the currently pending WHERE expression is passed to the program, where it can be either used or ignored.

Creating an Empty Lookup Table

Submit the following PROC SQL statements in the Program Editor to create an empty lookup table.

```
proc sql;
create table sasuser.lookup
  (lookltc  char(100) label='library.table.column',
   lookinfo char(200) label='varies depending on strategy',
   strategy char(8)   label='lookup strategy to use'
  );
```

SASUSER.LOOKUP is the default name of the lookup table. The SQL Query Window looks for this table to determine whether any automatic lookup is to be performed

Adding a Row to the Lookup Table

After you create the empty lookup table, you can submit additional PROC SQL statements to insert values into the table's LOOKLTC, LOOKINFO, and STRATEGY columns. You can also invoke PROC FSEDIT to add this information. The syntax for inserting values into the table is

```
proc sql;
insert into lookup.table
  values('lookltc-value','lookinfo-value','strategy-value');
```

Add a row to the SASUSER.LOOKUP data set by submitting the following code in the Program Editor:

```
proc sql;
insert into sasuser.lookup
  values('sample.empinfo.location','sample.program.region.frame','P');
quit;
```

This row contains information that the SQL Query Window uses to perform automatic lookup. Whenever the LOCATION column is selected from the SAMPLE.EMPINFO table in the WHERE EXPRESSION window for any query, the FRAME entry that is defined in SAMPLE.PROGRAM.REGION.FRAME is executed. The lookup strategy value of P indicates that the action that is to take place is a program execution.

Using the Lookup Table

Before you can use the lookup table, you do either of the following in order for the SQL Query Window to read the lookup table:

- □ exit and restart the SQL Query Window
- □ switch to a profile that uses SASUSER.LOOKUP as the automatic lookup table.

For this example, select**Tools ▶ Switch to New Profile**. Select the SASUSER.PROFILE.QUERY profile and select [OK]. The SASUSER.PROFILE.QUERY profile uses SASUSER.LOOKUP as the automatic lookup table.

To display the number of employees in each division within a specific geographic region, from the SQL QUERY TABLES window, select **File ▶ List/Include Saved Queries** to display the Saved Queries window.

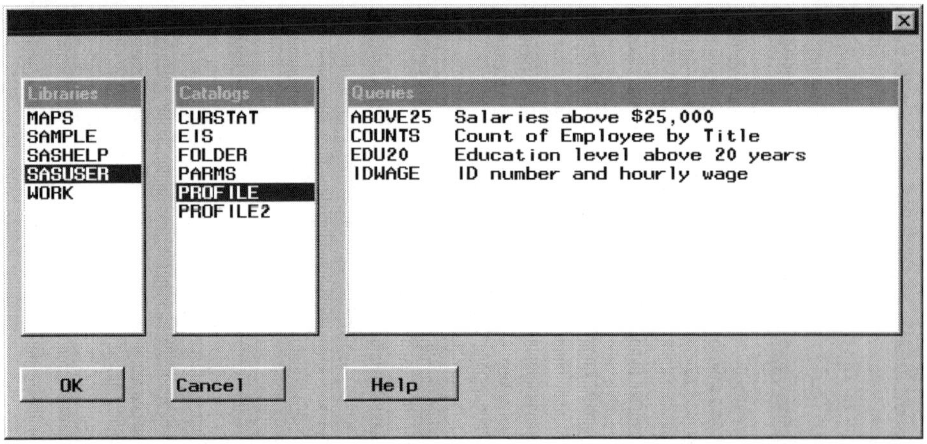

Select **SASUSER.PROFILE.COUNTS**, which you created in “Counting and Grouping Data Automatically” on page 45. Select [OK] to include the query and to return to the SQL QUERY TABLES window.

Select **View ▶ Where Conditions for Subset** to display the WHERE EXPRESSION window.

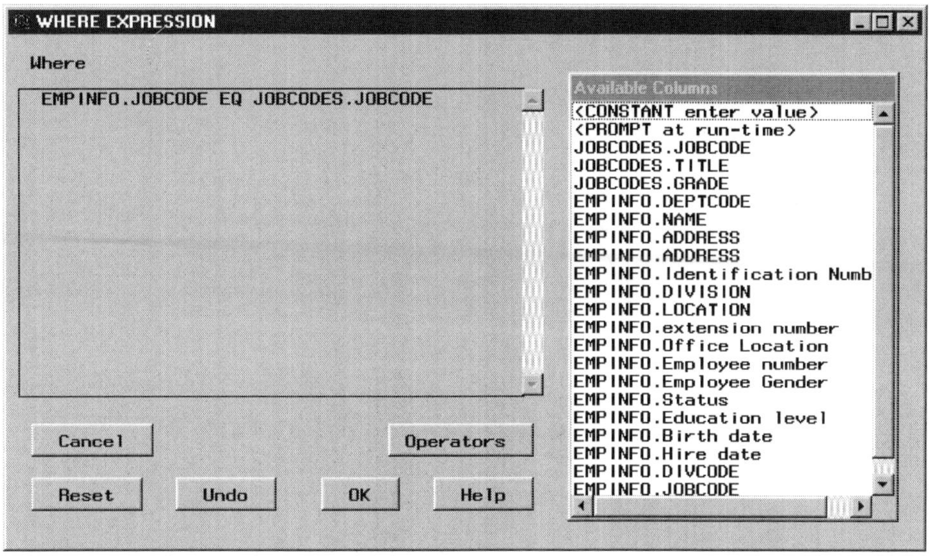

Select [Operators]. Select **AND** from the list of operators.

Select **EMPINFO.LOCATION** from the Available Columns list. Select **EQ** from the list of comparison operators that appears. Because you have defined EMPINFO.LOCATION with an automatic lookup, the Company Locations window automatically appears.

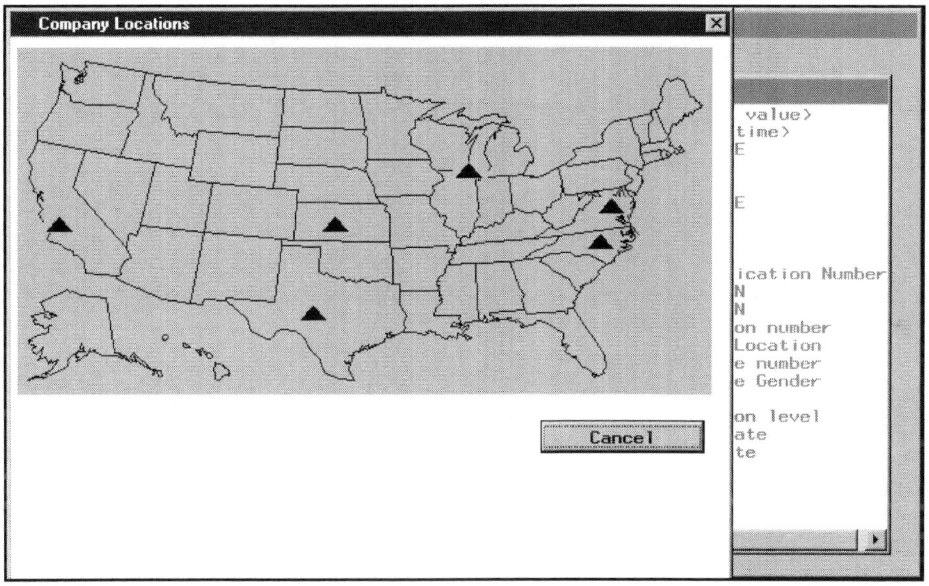

The Company Locations window is the FRAME entry that is defined in SAMPLE.PROGRAM.REGION.FRAME. Select the westernmost site to complete the WHERE clause.

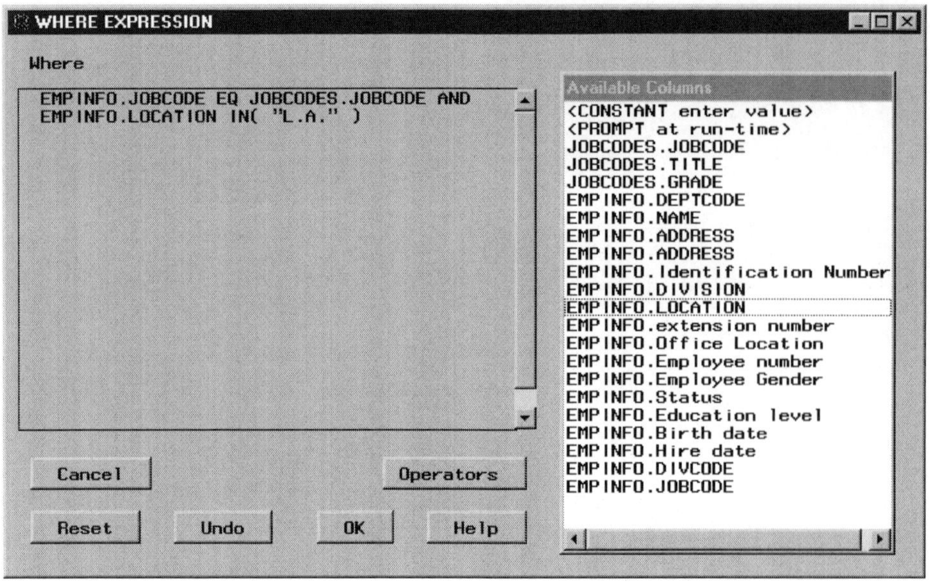

Select [OK].

Viewing Your Output

Select **Tools ▸ Run Query ▸ Run Immediate** to display the results of your query.

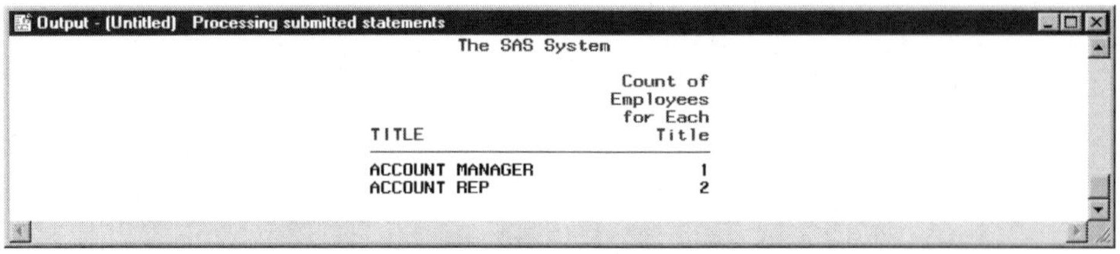

In the SQL QUERY TABLES window, select **Tools ▸ Reset** to reset your query. Select [OK] from the dialog box that appears.

Using a Slider Bar to Indicate a Range

You can use a slider bar to select a range of lookup values in a query.

In this example, you associate the slider with the EMPINFO.SALARY column. Because you might not want to permanently associate these lookup values with the EMPINFO.SALARY column, you can insert the lookup table into a different profile and switch to that profile when you want to use the slider bar.

Creating a New Lookup Table

Submit the following PROC SQL statements in the Program Editor to create an empty lookup table in the SAMPLE library.

```
proc sql;
create table sample.lookup
  (lookltc  char(100) label='library.table.column',
```

```
    lookinfo char(200) label='varies depending on strategy',
    strategy char(8)   label='lookup strategy to use'
   );
```

Add a row to the SAMPLE.LOOKUP data set by submitting the following code in the Program Editor:

```
proc sql;
insert into sample.lookup
  values('sample.salary.salary','sample.program.salrange.frame','P');
quit;
```

SAMPLE.PROGRAM.SALRANGE.FRAME is a FRAME entry that defines the slider bar.

Creating a New Profile

Create an SQL Query Window profile that specifies SAMPLE.LOOKUP as the automatic lookup table as follows. Select **Profile ▸ Set Preferences**.

Select the right arrow next to Automatic Lookup to display the Set Lookup SAS Data Set for Preferences window.

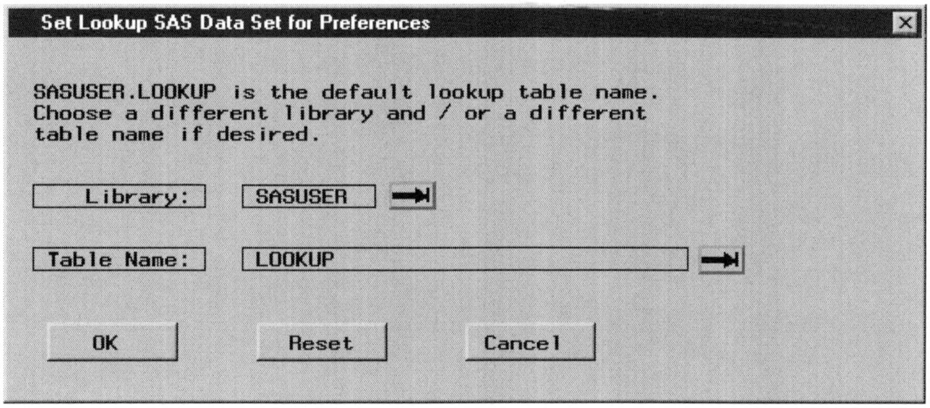

Select the right arrow next to the Library field. Select **`SAMPLE`** from the Libraries list and select [OK]. Select [OK] to return to the Preference Settings for Profile window.

Select the right arrow next to Data Restrictions to display the Data Restrictions for Profile window. Select **`SAMPLE`** from the Table Sources list. Select **`Add entire Table Source to preferences`** from the pop-up menu that appears. Select **`WORK`** from the Table Sources list. Select **`Add entire Table Source to preferences`** from the pop-up menu that appears.

Note: If you do not have write access to the SAMPLE library, then repeat the previous step for the SASUSER library. △

Select [OK] to return to the Preference Settings for Profile window.

Select [Save] to save your new profile setting. Type **`LOOKUP`** in the Entry Name field of the Name Catalog Entry for Profile window. Type **`Slider Bar for Salary Range`** in the description field.

Select [OK] to return to the Preference Settings for Profile window. Select [Close].

From the SQL QUERY TABLES window, select **Tools ▸ Switch to New Profile**. The Preference Profiles in Catalog window appears.

Select the right arrow next to the Profile Name field to display a list of profiles. Select the **`SASUSER.PROFILE.LOOKUP`** profile.

Select [OK] to return to the SQL QUERY TABLES window and to complete the switch to the new profile.

See “Setting Your Profile” on page 69 for more information about the SQL Query Window user profile.

A Demonstration of the Slider Bar

To show how the slider works, you can construct a simple WHERE expression that displays the range of salaries. In the SQL QUERY TABLES window, select SAMPLE.SALARY from the Available Tables list and add it to the Selected Tables list. Select [OK] to display the SQL QUERY COLUMNS window.

In the SQL QUERY COLUMNS window, select **Salary** and **Identification Number** from the Available Columns list and add them to the Selected Columns list.

Select **View ▶ Where Conditions for Subset**.

In the WHERE EXPRESSION window, select **Salary** from the Available Columns list. Select **Between** from the OTHER Operators list. Because the lookup table is associated with the Salary column, the slider bar that is the FRAME entry appears.

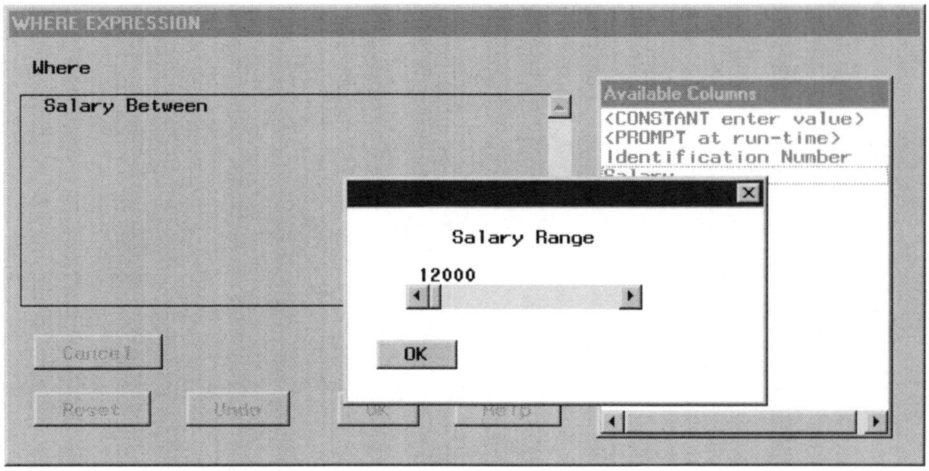

Select [OK] to accept the value of **12000**. The slider bar appears again because the Between operator requires a second value. Move the slider to the right until **51000** is displayed. Select [OK] to complete the WHERE expression.

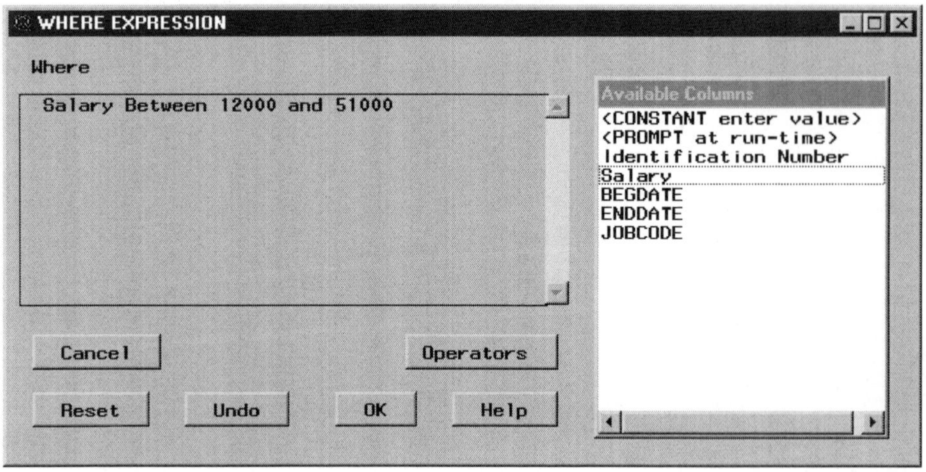

Select [OK] to return to the SQL QUERY COLUMNS window. Select **Tools ▶ Run Query ▶ Run Immediate** to display the employee identification numbers whose salaries are between $12,000 and $51,000.

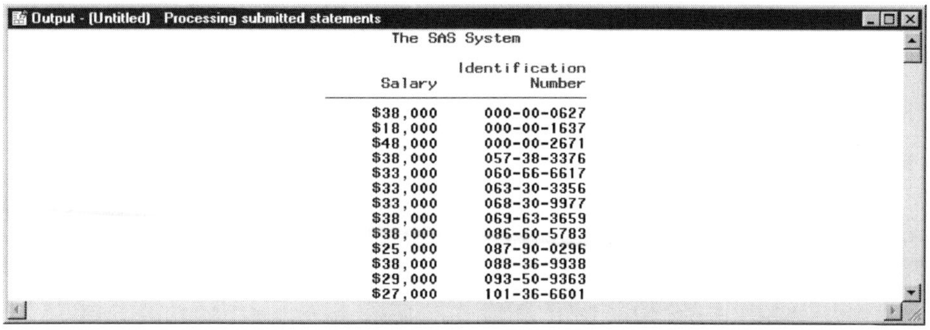
Output - (Untitled) Processing submitted statements

The SAS System

Salary	Identification Number
$38,000	000-00-0627
$18,000	000-00-1637
$48,000	000-00-2671
$38,000	057-38-3376
$33,000	060-66-6617
$33,000	063-30-3356
$33,000	068-30-9977
$38,000	069-63-3659
$38,000	086-60-5783
$25,000	087-90-0296
$38,000	088-36-9938
$29,000	093-50-9363
$27,000	101-36-6601

Select **Tools ▶ Reset** to reset the query and return to the SQL QUERY TABLES window.

Using SCL to Call a FRAME Entry

If your site is licensed to use SAS/AF software, then you can use SAS Component Language (SCL) to create a lookup table that uses the SAMPLE.PROGRAM.SALRANGE.FRAME entry or another FRAME entry that you design. The following SCL program is associated with the SAMPLE.PROGRAM.SALRANGE.FRAME entry:

```
entry looklst 8 lkuptype $1 rc 8 msg $40 wherelst 8;

init:
 salrange =12000;
 lkuptype = 'N';
return;


main:
return;

term:
return;

range:
  call notify('range', '_GET_VALUE_', value);
  call notify('salrange', '_SET_VALUE_', value);
return;

ok:
 call notify('salrange', '_GET_VALUE_', value);
 looklst  = insertn(looklst, value, 1);
 rc       = 0;
 _status_ = 'H';
 link term;
return;
```

Refer to *SAS Component Language: Reference* for more information about SCL.

Creating and Using Outer Joins

An outer join combines rows of data from two tables. There are three types of outer joins:

left join
: returns all matching rows in both tables, in addition to rows in the left table that have no matching rows in the right table.

right join
: returns all matching rows in both tables, in addition to rows in the right table that have no matching rows in the left table.

full join
: returns all matching and nonmatching rows from both tables.

In all three types of outer joins, the columns in the result row that are from the unmatched row are set to missing values.

In this example, you first create an inner join that relates employee identification number and salary. Then, you create an outer join that combines this data with data from another table to compute the gross monthly pay for employees who have taken leave.

Creating a Query View

You can create an SQL view that contains the syntax of your query. For this example, you use a view to create an outer join query.

In the SQL QUERY TABLES window, select **SAMPLE.EMPINFO** and **SAMPLE.SALARY** from the Available Tables list and add them to the Selected Tables list. Select [OK].

In the SQL QUERY COLUMNS window, select **NAME**, the two **ADDRESS** items, **Identification Number**, **Employee number**, **Salary**, **BEGDATE**, and **ENDDATE** and add them to the Selected Columns list.

Select **View ▶ Where Conditions for Subset** to display the WHERE EXPRESSION window.

Select **EMPINFO.Identification Number** from the Available Columns list. Select **EQ** from the list of operators. Select **Salary.Identification Number** from the Available Columns list. Select [OK].

This WHERE expression creates an inner join of EMPINFO and Salary based on Identification Number. To save the query as a view, select **Tools ▶ Show Query** to display the SQL QUERY window. Select [Create View].

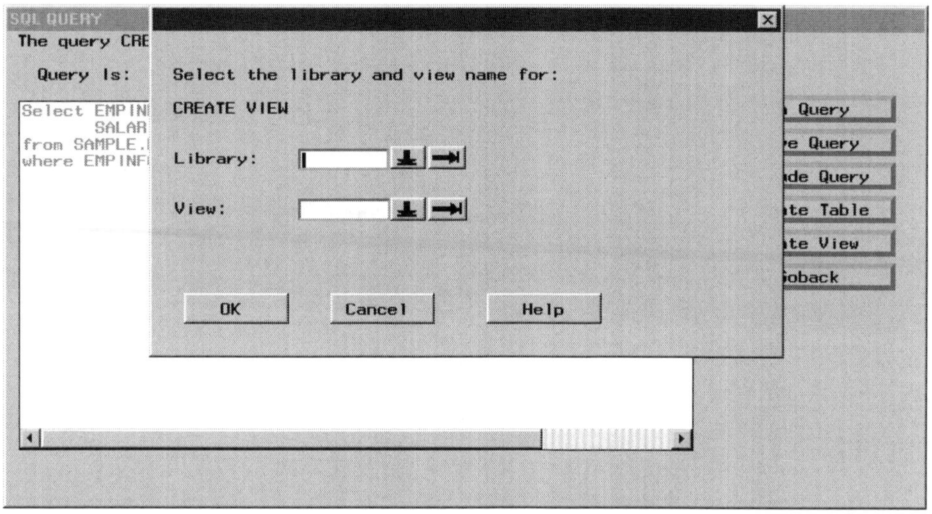

Select the right arrow next to the Library field to display a list of SAS libraries.

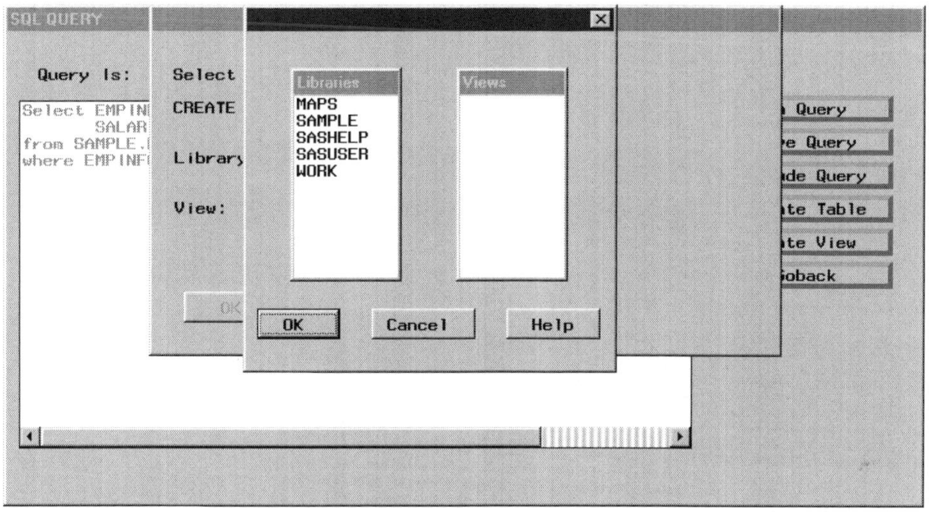

The list of libraries displayed at your site might be different from the ones in the illustration. Select **SAMPLE** from the Libraries list. Select [OK].

Type **MYVIEW** in the View field. Select [OK] to return to the SQL QUERY window. Select [Goback] to return to the SQL QUERY COLUMNS window.

Creating an Outer Join

Select **Tools ▶ Reset** to reset the query. Select [OK] in the dialog box that appears.

Select **SAMPLE.MYVIEW** and **SAMPLE.LEAVE** from the Available Tables list and add them to the Selected Tables list. Select [OK] to display the SQL QUERY COLUMNS window.

Select **View ▶ Join Type**.

Select **Matched Join and Unmatched Rows (Outer Join)**. Select [OK] to display the Columns for Setting Join Criteria window.

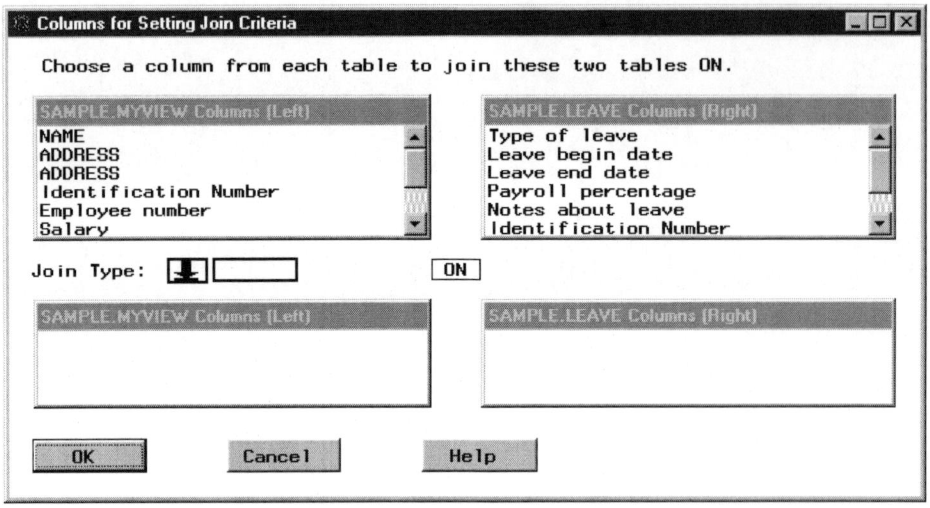

Select **Identification Number** from the SAMPLE.MYVIEW Columns (Left) list. Select **Identification Number** from the SAMPLE.LEAVE Columns (Right) list. Select the down arrow next to Join Type. Select **Left** from the pop-up menu. Select OK to return to the SQL QUERY COLUMNS window.

Select **View ▶ Distinct** to eliminate duplicate values from your output.

Select **NAME**, **Identification Number**, and **Employee number** from the Available Columns list and add them to the Selected Columns list.

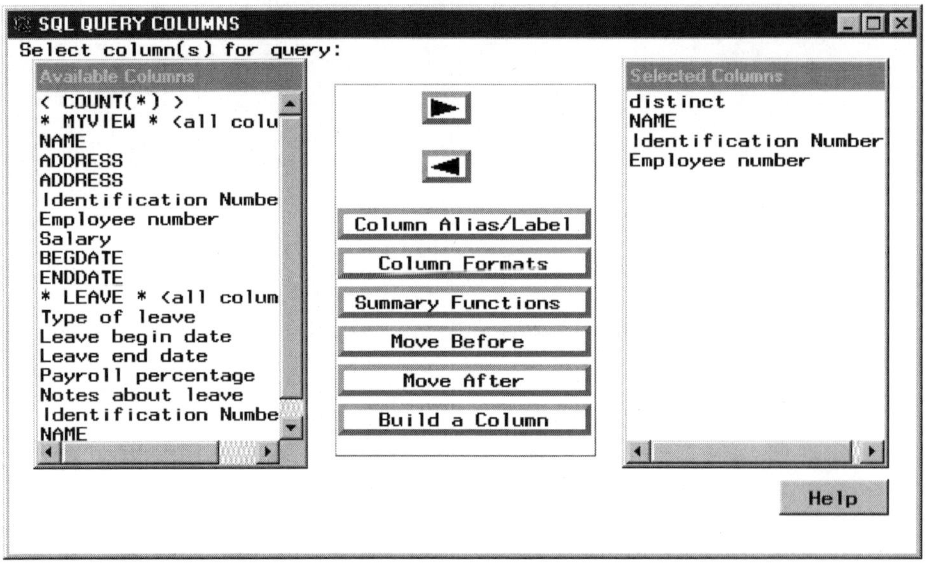

Building a Column Expression

Select Build a Column to display the BUILD A COLUMN EXPRESSION window.

Select **MYVIEW.Salary** from the Available Columns list. Select **/** from the list of operators. Select **<CONSTANT enter value>** from the Available Columns list. Type **12** in the Numeric field. Select OK. Select outside the list of operators to dismiss it.

Select **Column Attributes** to display the Expression Column Attributes window. Enter **monthpay** in the Alias Name field. Enter **dollar12.2** in the Format field. Enter **Employee's Monthly Pay** in the Label field.

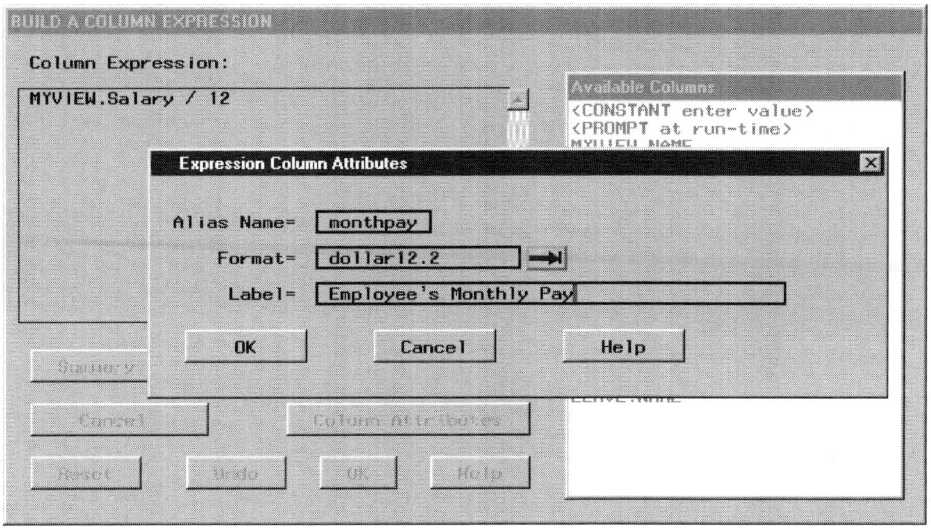

Select [OK] to return to the BUILD A COLUMN EXPRESSION window. Select OK to return to the SQL QUERY COLUMNS window.

In the SQL QUERY COLUMNS window, select [Build a Column] to display the BUILD A COLUMN EXPRESSION window. Select [Operators]. Select **(** from the list of operators.

Select **monthpay** from the Available Columns list. Select * from the list of operators. Select **LEAVE.Payroll percentage** from the Available Columns list. Select **)** from the list of operators. Select outside the list of operators to dismiss it.

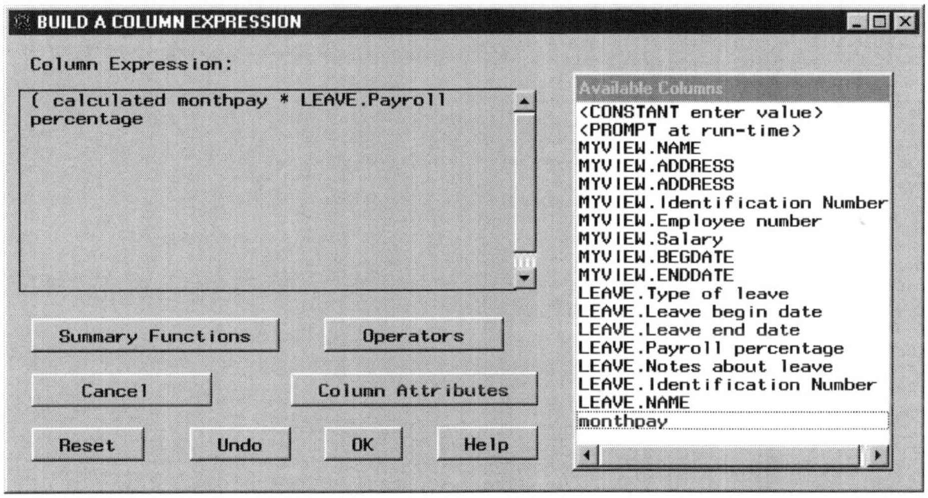

Select [Column Attributes] to display the Expression Column Attributes window. Enter **adjstpay** in the Alias Name field. Enter **dollar12.2** in the Format field. Enter **Employee's Gross Pay** in the Label field. Select [OK] to return to the BUILD A COLUMN EXPRESSION window. Select [OK] to return to the SQL QUERY COLUMNS window.

Order By Columns

In the SQL QUERY COLUMNS window, select **View ▶ Order By** to display the ORDER BY COLUMNS window.

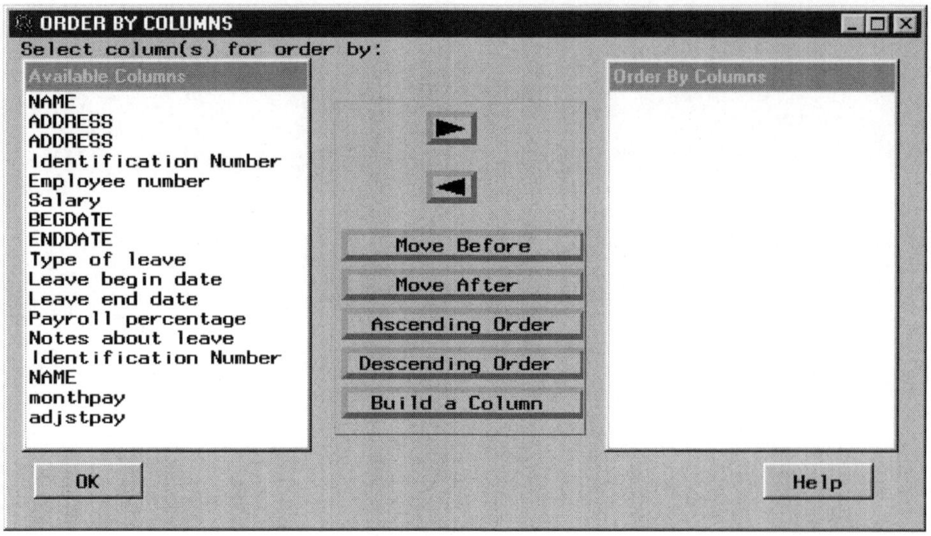

Select the second **`Identification Number`** from the Available Columns list and add it to the Order By Columns list. Select OK to return to the SQL QUERY COLUMNS window.

Viewing Your Output

Select **Tools ▸ Run Query ▸ Run Immediate** to display the results of the query in the Output window.

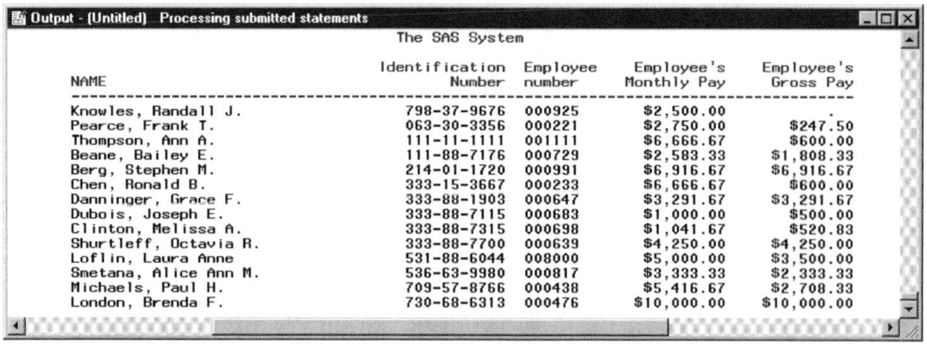

The SAS System

NAME	Identification Number	Employee number	Employee's Monthly Pay	Employee's Gross Pay
Knowles, Randall J.	798-37-9676	000925	$2,500.00	.
Pearce, Frank T.	063-30-3356	000221	$2,750.00	$247.50
Thompson, Ann A.	111-11-1111	001111	$6,666.67	$600.00
Beane, Bailey E.	111-88-7176	000729	$2,583.33	$1,808.33
Berg, Stephen M.	214-01-1720	000991	$6,916.67	$6,916.67
Chen, Ronald B.	333-15-3667	000233	$6,666.67	$600.00
Danninger, Grace F.	333-88-1903	000647	$3,291.67	$3,291.67
Dubois, Joseph E.	333-88-7115	000683	$1,000.00	$500.00
Clinton, Melissa A.	333-88-7315	000698	$1,041.67	$520.83
Shurtleff, Octavia R.	333-88-7700	000639	$4,250.00	$4,250.00
Loflin, Laura Anne	531-88-6044	008000	$5,000.00	$3,500.00
Smetana, Alice Ann M.	536-63-9980	000817	$3,333.33	$2,333.33
Michaels, Paul H.	709-57-8766	000438	$5,416.67	$2,708.33
London, Brenda F.	730-68-6313	000476	$10,000.00	$10,000.00

CHAPTER 3

Customizing Your Session and Using Advanced Features

Setting Your Profile

You can customize your SQL Query Window sessions by specifying your own default settings and storing them in a profile. When you invoke the SQL Query Window with the profile, your own preferences are automatically in effect. Your user-defined default settings are called preference settings. You can set up customized profiles for yourself or for a group of users. For example, you can define a profile to specify which table sources and tables are available in an SQL Query Window session.

Create a profile entry by selecting, from the SQL Query Window,**Profile ▶ Set Preferences**.

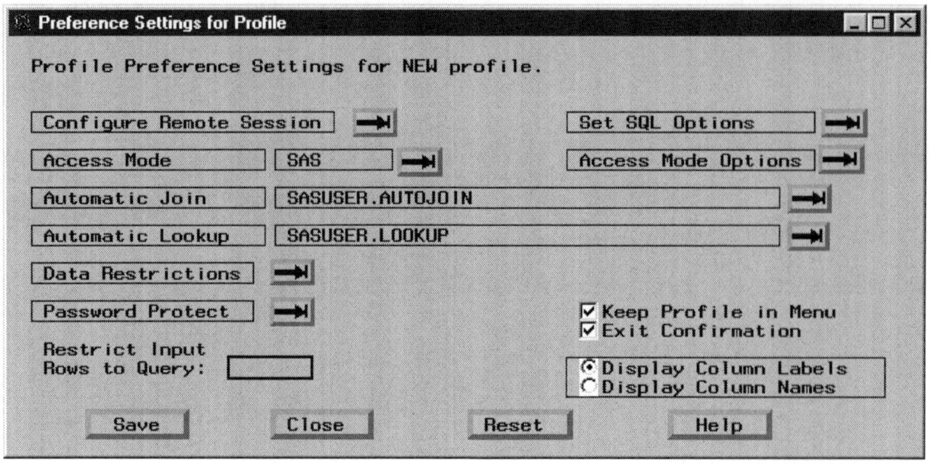

Configure Remote Session

Installations that license SAS/CONNECT software can use the SQL Query Window to query tables or databases that are stored on remote systems. To connect to a remote system you must first create an SQL Query Window profile that contains information about the remote configuration.

Select the right arrow next to Configure Remote Session in the Preference Settings for Profile window.

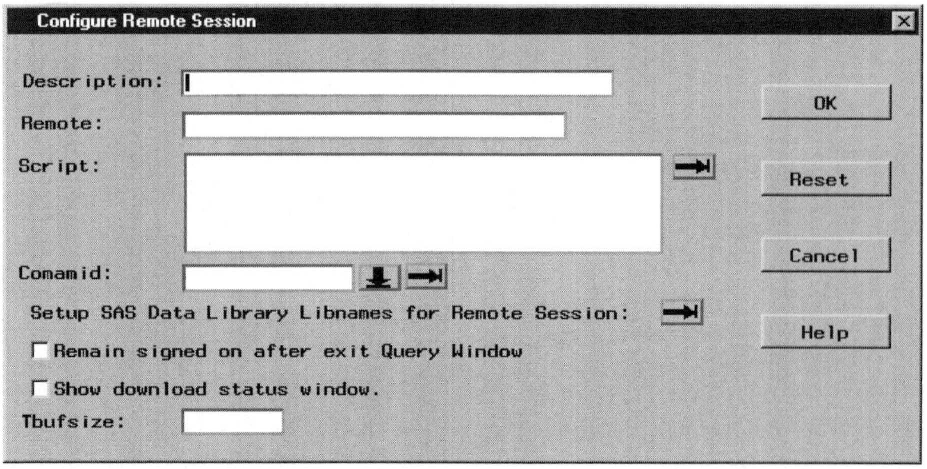

Fill in the fields in this window with values that are appropriate for your site.

Use the Description field to describe the remote configuration.

Select the right arrow next to Setup SAS Data Library Libnames for Remote Session to enter the values that will be used to submit SAS statements remotely.

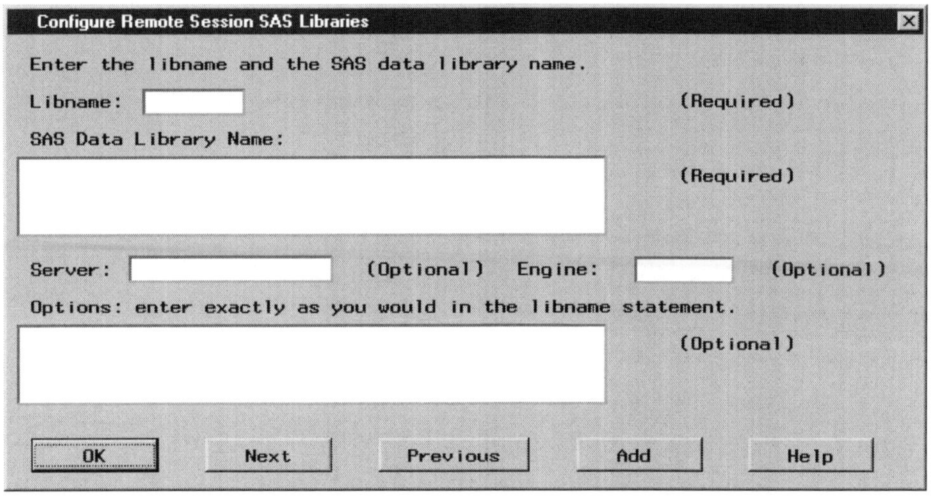

To query DBMS data through a SAS/ACCESS library engine, enter the name of the libref that you want to create in the Libname field. Enter the name of the SAS/ACCESS library engine that you want to use (usually the DBMS name) in the Engine field. Enter the LIBNAME options that are required for the libref in the Options field. In most cases, the SAS Data Library Name field can remain empty. For more information about library engines, see the SAS/ACCESS software documentation for your DBMS.

When you have entered your values, select [OK] to return to the Configure Remote Session window. Select [OK] to return to the Profile Preference Settings window.

Use the other items in the Profile Preference Settings window to specify any other preference settings that you want to include in your profile.

Select [Save] to save the profile.

Signing On to the Remote Host

You can sign on to the remote host either when you invoke the SQL Query Window, or during an SQL Query Window session.

- To sign on to the remote host when you invoke the SQL Query Window, specify the profile that contains the remote configuration information. The connection to the remote host is made automatically.
- To sign on to the remote host during an SQL Query Window session, select **Tools ▶ Switch to New Profile**. In the Switch to New Profile window, specify the library, catalog name, and profile name for the profile that contains your remote configuration information. Select [OK] to make the connection to the remote host.
- To remain signed on after exiting the SQL Query Window, select **`Remain signed on after exit Query Window`** in the Configure Remote Session window. If the remote host that is specified in your profile has already been signed on to during your SAS session, then the SQL Query Window uses that connection to the remote host. You are not signed off from the remote host when you exit the SQL Query Window session.

Access Mode

Access Mode specifies the source of the data that you will access. The source can be either SAS (for SAS data files and views), or most of the database management systems (DBMSs) for which the PROC SQL Pass-Through Facility is available if you have SAS/ACCESS software installed. If you are using a SAS/ACCESS library engine to query DBMS data, then set the access mode to SAS. This mode enables you to access the DBMS data via the libraries that are defined in your SAS session. The default access mode is SAS.

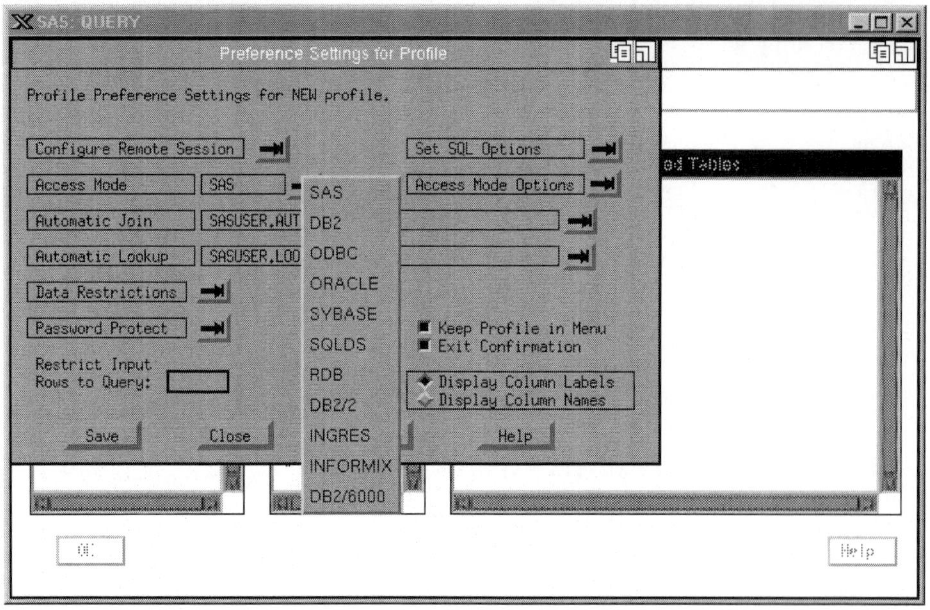

Access Mode Options

For some DBMSs, such as Sybase and ORACLE, you must specify access mode options such as the user name, password, and server. When you select one of these DBMSs that require options from the Access Mode window, an Access Mode Options window appears.

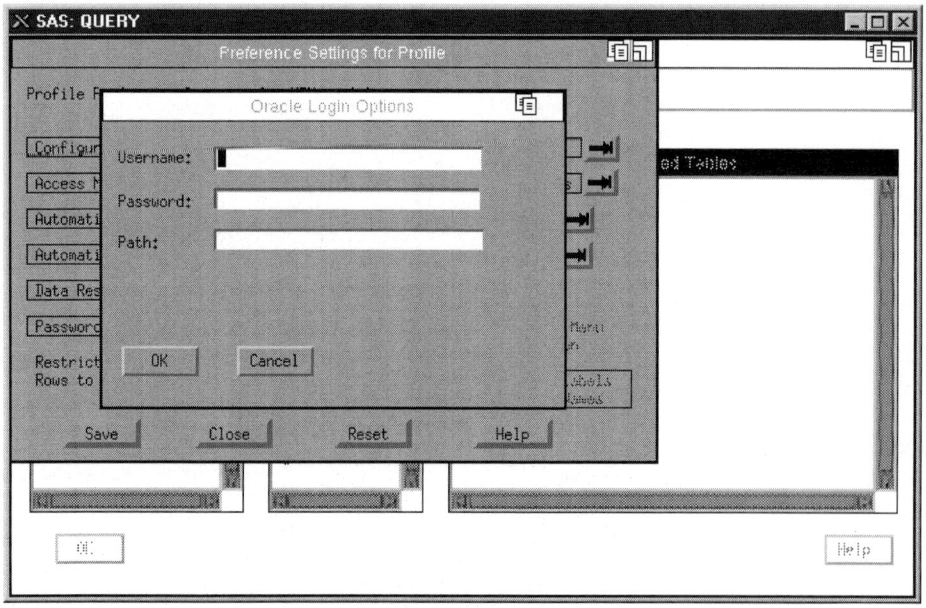

For access modes such as DB2 that do not require any options, you can select **`Access Mode Options`** to set additional options.

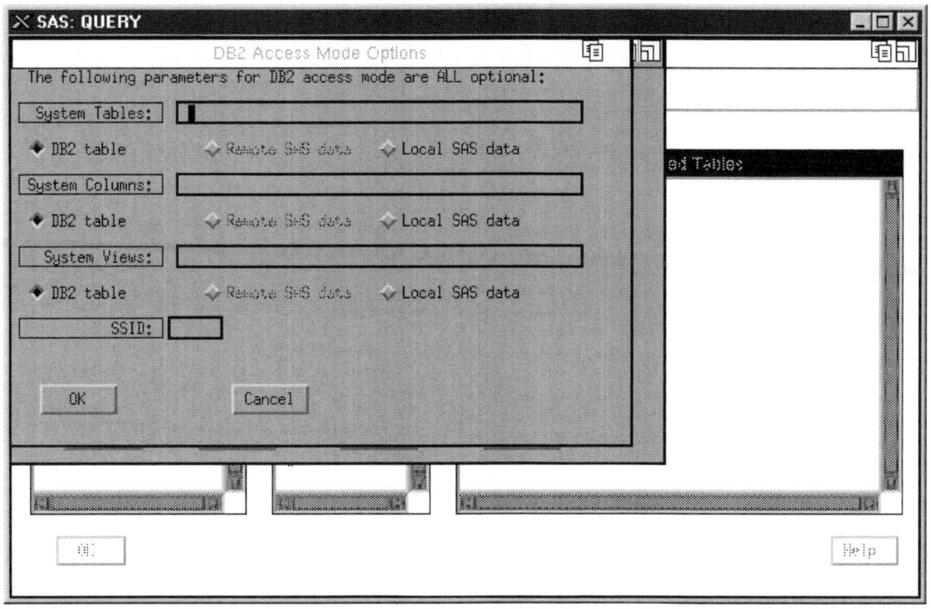

Automatic Join

An automatic join (or "autojoin") data set contains the table names and column links that are required to join tables automatically in an SQL Query Window session. When tables that are defined in the automatic join data set are selected together, the corresponding column links are used to automatically start the query's WHERE expression. An autojoin data set can be shared by many users.

Creating an Automatic Join Data Set

The following example illustrates the creation of an automatic join data set. Select the right arrow next to the Automatic Join field, and then select **`Create an Automatic Join Data Set`** from the pop-up menu that appears.

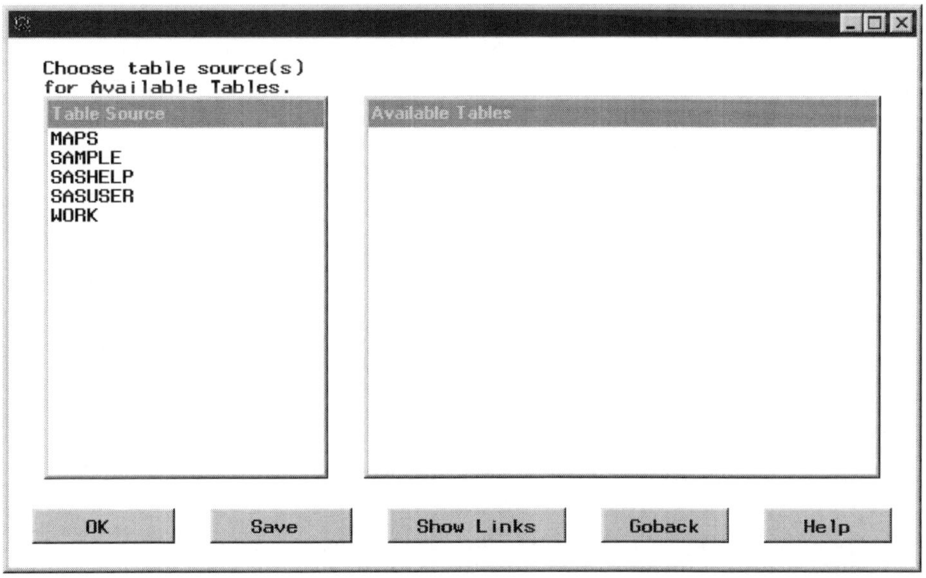

Select **SAMPLE** from the Table Source list to populate the Available Tables list. Select SAMPLE.EMPINFO and SAMPLE.LEAVE. Select OK. The Automatic Join Column Links window is displayed.

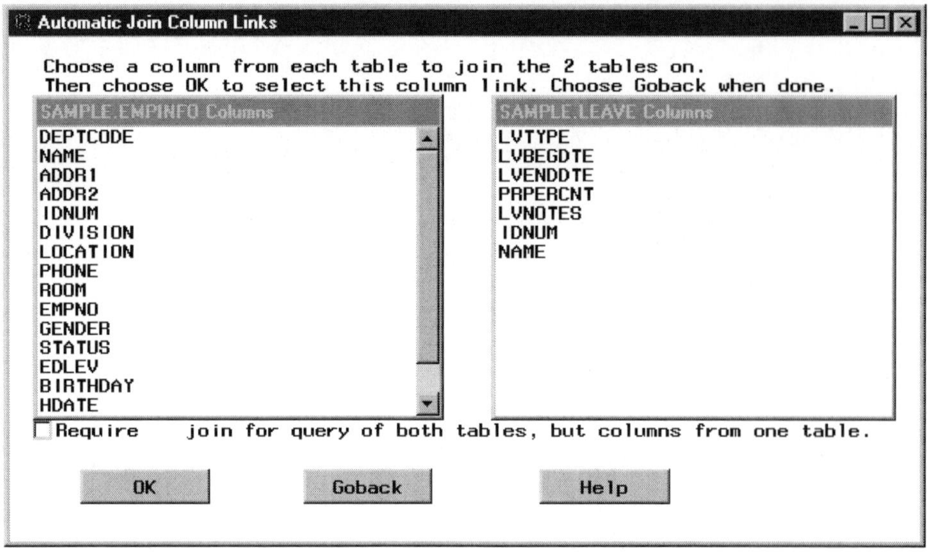

These two tables have the NAME column in common. Select NAME from both the SAMPLE.EMPINFO Columns list and the SAMPLE.LEAVE Columns list. Select OK. If the two tables had any other columns in common, then you would be able to select these columns as well and store the column links in the automatic join data set.

Select Goback to return to the Available Tables list.

Select Show Links to display the link that you have created between the two data sets.

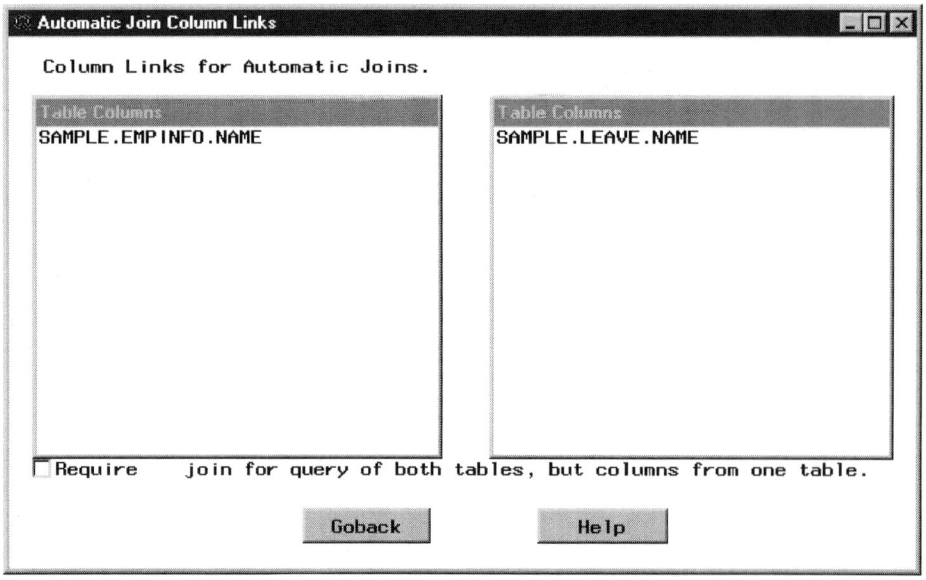

Select Goback. You can repeat the previous procedure for as many pairs of tables as you want.

When you are finished defining column links, select Save to save your automatic join data set.

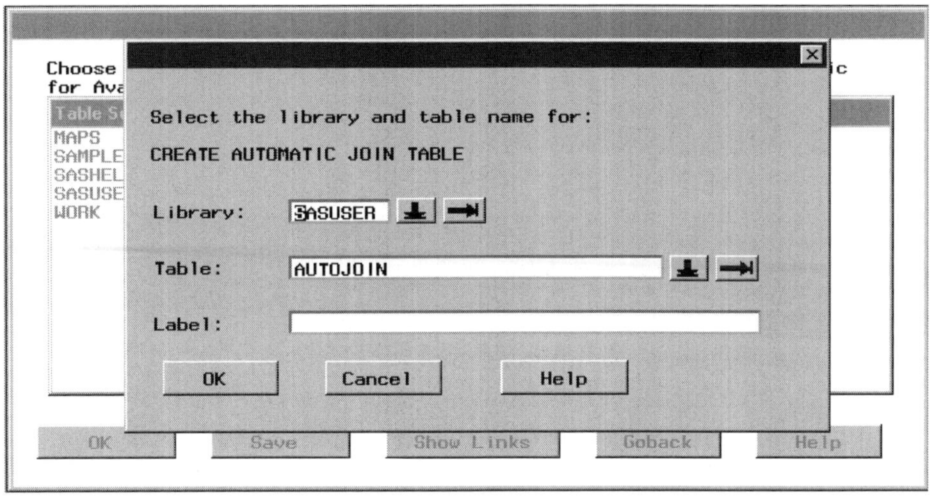

If desired, type an appropriate label in the Label field. Select OK.

Note: For this example, the default SASUSER.AUTOJOIN data set is used. However, by specifying a different library or table name, you can save the autojoin data set to a different location. △

Select Goback to return to the Preference Settings for Profile window. Select Save and then OK to save the changes to the profile. Select Close to return to the SQL QUERY TABLES window.

When you start the SQL Query Window, the software looks for the automatic join data set that is specified in the default profile, whether the automatic join data set is the default SASUSER.AUTOJOIN or some other data set that you have specified. If an autojoin data set is not found, then no automatic joins are performed.

Select **File ▸ Close** to end your SQL Query Window session. Select OK in the dialog box that appears in order to return to the Program Editor.

Invoke another SQL Query Window session. Select SAMPLE.EMPINFO and SAMPLE.LEAVE from the Available Tables list and add them to the Selected Tables list. Select OK to display the SQL QUERY COLUMNS window.

Select DIVISION from the Available Columns list and add it to the Selected Columns list.

Select **View ▸ Where Conditions for Subset** to display the WHERE EXPRESSION window.

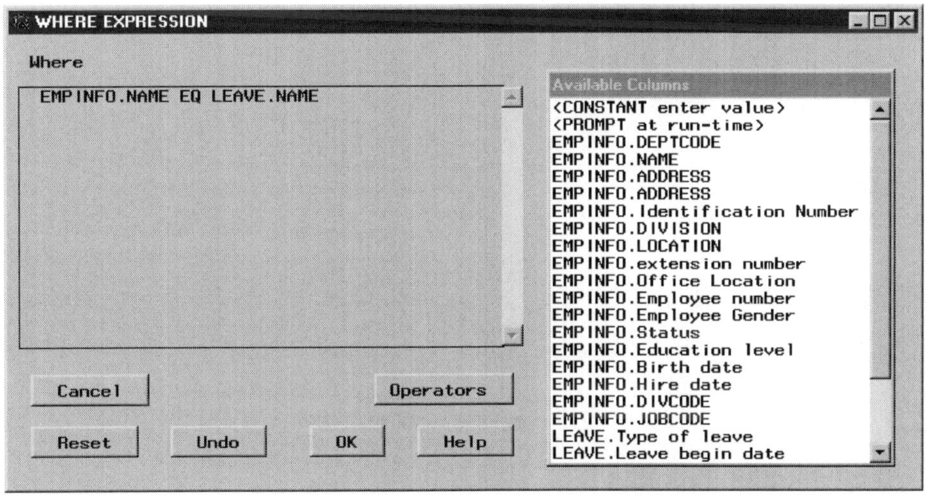

The WHERE expression begins with the column link that you specified in your autojoin table.

Updating Your Automatic Join Data Set

You can update an automatic join data set with PROC FSEDIT or PROC SQL. Automatic join data sets contain two columns, AUTOCOL1 and AUTOCOL2. Each column contains the library name, table name, and column name, in the format **`libname.table-name.column-name`**, for one of the column links.

Selecting a Different Automatic Join Data Set

You can select a different automatic join data set for a given profile. In the Preference Settings for Profile window, select the right arrow next to the Automatic Join field, then select **`Set Name for Automatic Join Data Set`** from the pop-up menu that appears. Select the library and table name of the desired autojoin data set and select [OK].

Automatic Lookup

Automatic Lookup specifies a lookup table. See "Using the Automatic Lookup Feature" on page 56 for information about the automatic lookup feature.

Data Restrictions

Data Restrictions specifies the table sources, tables, and columns that will be available in an SQL Window session that is invoked with this profile. Data Restrictions also shows you which table sources, tables, and columns you have made available for the profile.

Password Protect

Password Protect enables you to specify a password for your profile. After you enter the password, you are prompted to re-enter it for verification. Thereafter, users can invoke the SQL Query Window with this profile without knowing the password. However, a user cannot update the profile without supplying the password.

Restrict Input Rows to Query

Restrict Input Rows to Query imposes a limit on the number of rows (observations) that the SQL Query Window will process from any single table. This item is useful for debugging queries on large tables, or for preventing the excessive expenditure of computer resources that would result from running queries on large tables.

Set SQL Options

Set SQL Options enables you to set SQL options for the execution of the query.

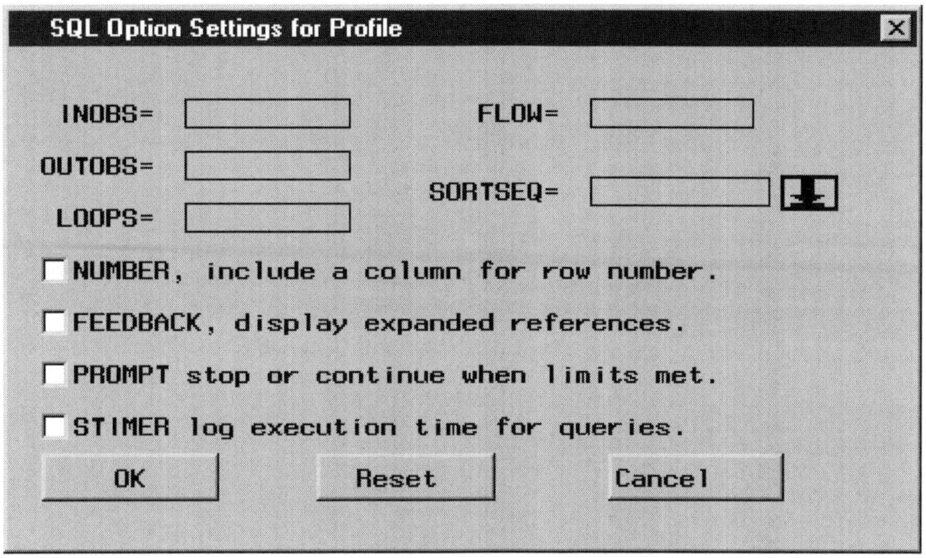

INOBS=
: restricts the number of rows that are processed from any single source.

OUTOBS=
: restricts the number of rows that are processed as the target.

LOOPS=
: limits the number of iterations in the inner loop.

FLOW=
: specifies the limit beyond which character columns are to be flowed to multiple lines.

SORTSEQ=
: specifies the collating sequence to be used with an ORDER BY clause. Use this option to specify a collating sequence other than the default.

Keep Profile in Menu

Keep Profile in Menu enables you to remove or retain the **`Profile`** item on the SQL Query Window menu bar and to turn on or off the ability to switch to a new profile from the **`Tools`** menu.

Exit Confirmation

Exit Confirmation enables you to turn off the dialog box that asks you if you want to end the query session. The dialog box appears when you select [Close] from the **`File`** menu.

Switching to Another Profile

To change to a different profile during an SQL Query Window session, select **Tools ▸ Switch to New Profile**.

In the dialog box that appears, select the library, catalog, and profile name for the desired profile. Select OK when you are finished making selections.

Handling Missing Values

You can use the SQL Query Window to test for missing values in a data set. This example generates a list of employees whose education level is not known.

From the SQL QUERY TABLES window, select SAMPLE.EMPINFO from the Available Tables list and add it to the Selected Tables list. Select OK.

In the SQL QUERY COLUMNS window, select **NAME** and **Education level** from the Available Columns list and add them to the Selected Columns list.

Select **View ▶ Where Conditions for Subset**.

In the WHERE EXPRESSION window, select **Education level** from the Available Columns list. Select **Is Missing** from the OTHER Operators list.

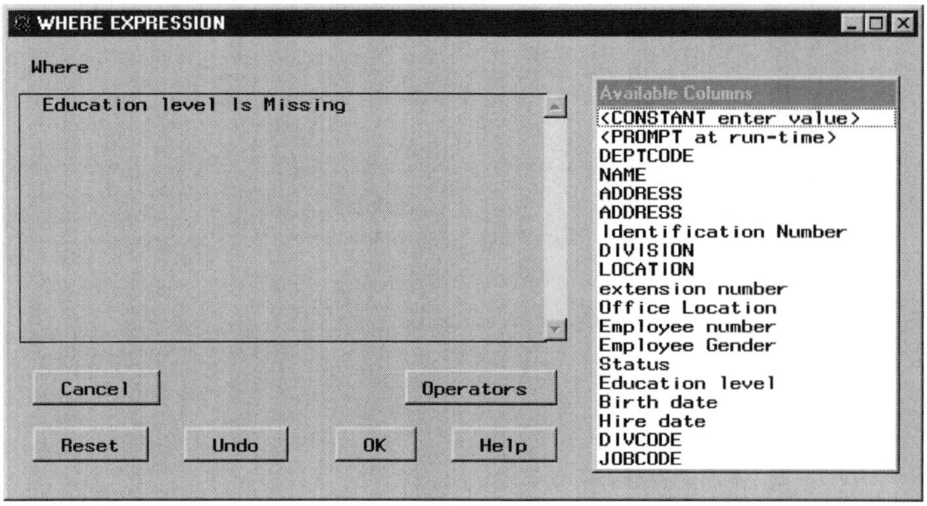

Select OK to return to the SQL QUERY COLUMNS window.

Select **Tools ▶ Run Query ▶ Run Immediate** to display a list of employees whose education level is missing from the data set.

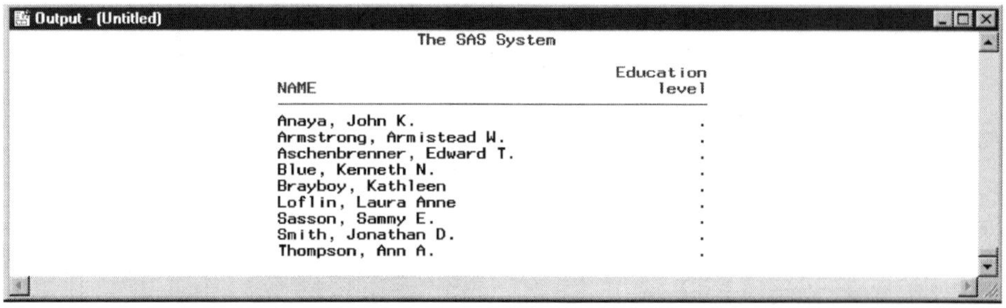

Defining a Format Outside the SQL Query Window

You can use the FORMAT procedure to define additional output formats. In this example, you define a format using the FORMAT procedure and then use that format to create a report with the SQL Query Window.

Creating the Format

In the Program Editor, submit the following SAS code:

```
proc format;
   value edlevel  1-12  = 'No High School Diploma'
                  12    = 'High School Diploma'
                  13    = 'Completing Associate'
                  14    = 'Associate'
                  15    = 'Completing Bachelors'
                  16    = 'Bachelors'
                  17    = 'Completing Masters'
                  18    = 'Masters'
                  19    = 'Completing PhD'
                  20-99 = 'PhD'
                  .     = 'No Education Data';
run;
```

The previous procedure creates the EDLEVEL. format, which prints a text string that corresponds to the numeric education level value.

See *Base SAS Procedures Guide* for more information about the FORMAT procedure.

Selecting Your Format

Invoke the SQL Query Window. In the SQL QUERY TABLES window, select SAMPLE.EMPINFO from the Available Tables list and add it to the Selected Tables list. Select OK.

In the SQL QUERY COLUMNS window, select **NAME** and **Education level** from the Available Columns List and add them to the Selected Columns list.

Select **Education level** from the Selected Columns list. Select Column Formats to display the Column Formats dialog box.

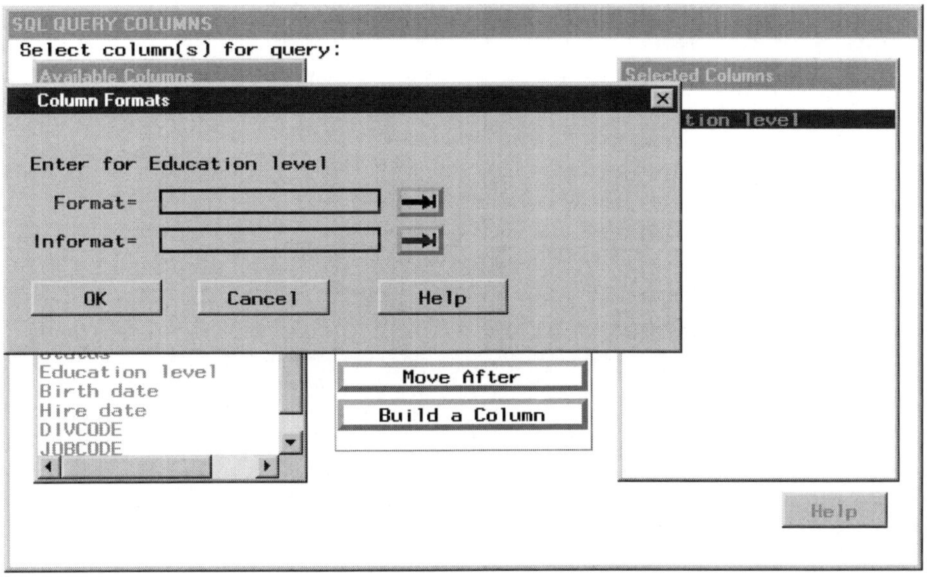

Select the right arrow next to the Format field to display the Format Names list.

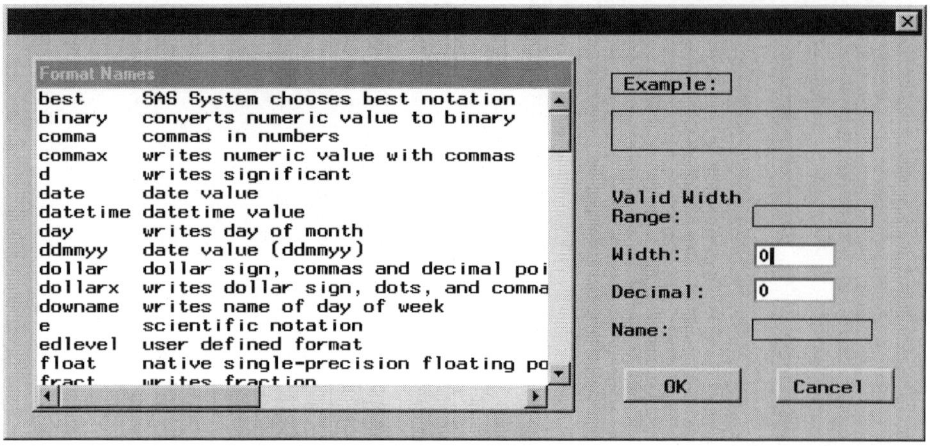

Select **edlevel** from the Format Names list. Select OK to return to the Column Formats window. Select OK to return to the SQL QUERY COLUMNS window.

Using Formatted Values in a WHERE Expression

Select **View ▸ Where Conditions for Subset** to display the WHERE EXPRESSION window. Select **Education level** from the Available Columns list. Select **EQ** from the list of operators.

Select **<LOOKUP distinct values>** from the Available Columns list. The Lookup Values list contains the distinct values for the Education Level column using the EDLEVEL. format that you defined.

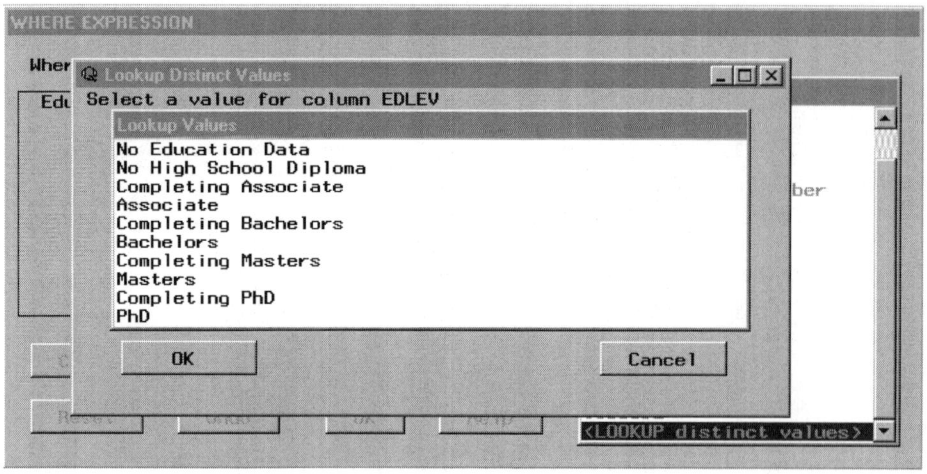

Select **PhD** from the list. Because the EQ operator can take only one value, the WHERE EXPRESSION window automatically reappears. Select OK to return to the SQL QUERY COLUMNS window.

Viewing Your Output

Select **Tools ▶ Run Query ▶ Run Immediate** to display a list of the employees whose education level is PhD.

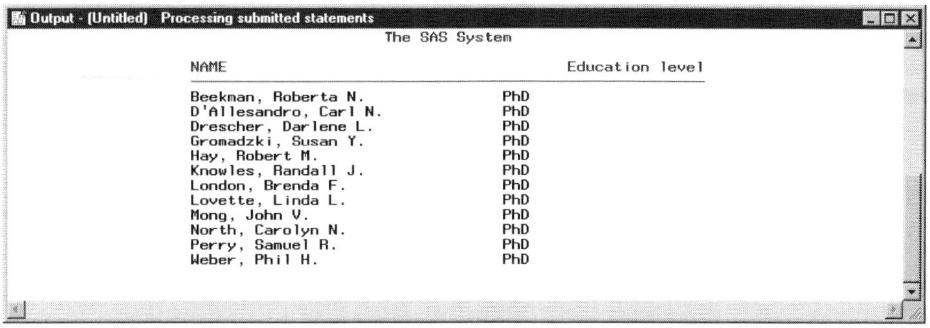

In the SQL QUERY COLUMNS window, select **Tools ▶ Reset** to reset the query. Select OK from the dialog box that appears.

Changing Access Modes

If you have the SAS/ACCESS interface to ORACLE installed, then you can switch access modes and use the SQL Pass-Through Facility to query ORACLE tables.

ORACLE Access Mode Options

From the SQL QUERY TABLES window, select **Tools ▶ Switch Access Mode ▶ ORACLE** to display the ORACLE Access Mode Options window.

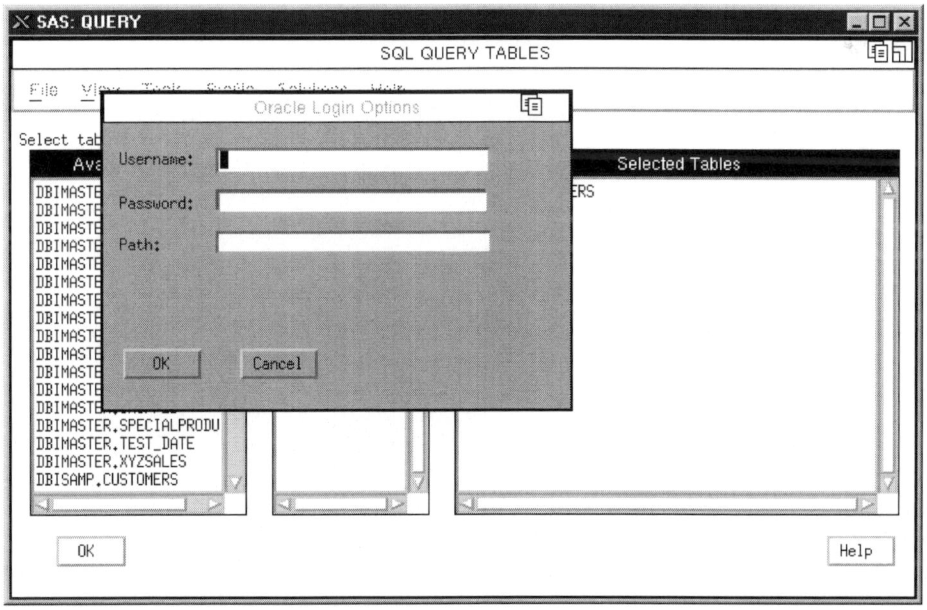

Fill in the fields with the information appropriate for your site. Contact your ORACLE administrator for more information.

Select OK to return to the SQL QUERY TABLES window. The sample tables that are available with your ORACLE DBMS are listed in the Available Tables column.

Creating a WHERE Expression

This example shows that although the steps for creating a WHERE expression are the same regardless of access mode, the generated SQL code is specific to the DBMS. If you have the SAS/ACCESS interface to ORACLE installed, then you can follow this example using any ORACLE table.

Select an ORACLE table from the Available Tables list and move it to the Selected Tables list. For this example, **ORDERS** is used. Select OK to display the SQL QUERY COLUMNS window.

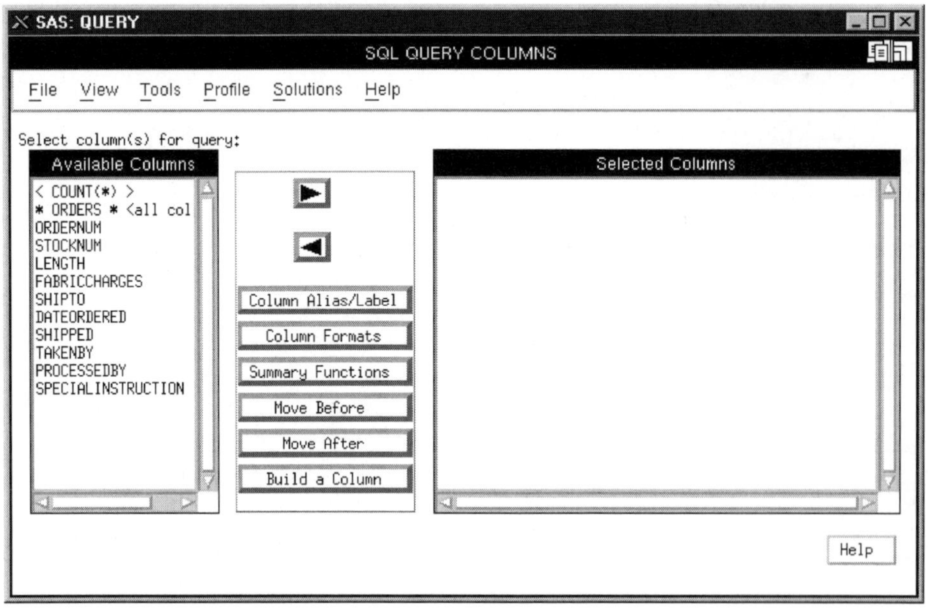

Select one or more columns from the Available Columns list and add them to the Selected Columns list. This example uses **FABRICCHARGES**, **SHIPTO**, **DATEORDERED**, **TAKENBY**, and **PROCESSEDBY**.

Select **View ▶ Where Conditions for Subset** to display the WHERE EXPRESSION window.

Create a WHERE expression. For this example, the expression **SHIPPED Is Not Missing** is created. Note that the **Is Not Missing** operator is selected from the OTHER Operators list.

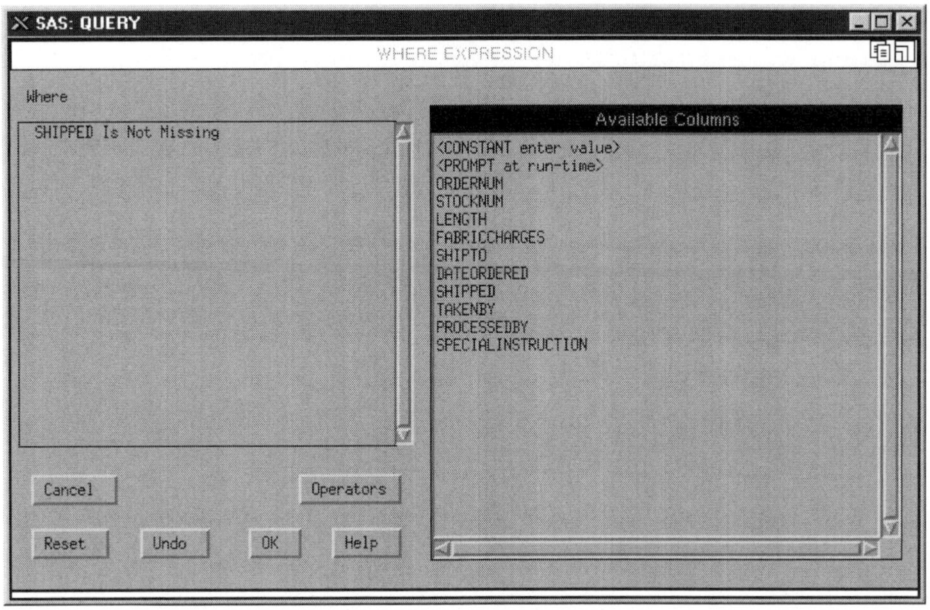

Select [OK] to close the WHERE EXPRESSION window.

Viewing Your Query

From the SQL QUERY COLUMNS window, select **Tools ▸ Show Query** to view your query.

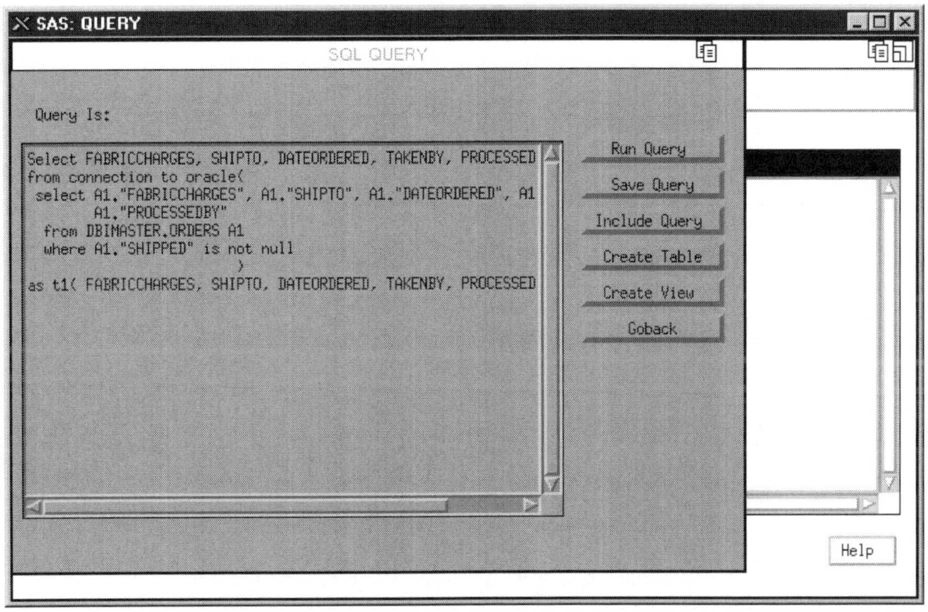

For this example, the query reports information for orders that have been shipped. ORACLE SQL is generated as the query is built.

The syntax that is enclosed by the parentheses that follow `from connection to oracle` is transported through the SQL Procedure Pass-Through Facility to the ORACLE DBMS for processing. The `Is Not Missing` operator from the WHERE expression is converted to the `is not null` ORACLE operator.

The syntax that is outside of the parentheses that follow **from connection to oracle** is processed by SAS.

Using SAS Data Sets to Store System Tables Information

For access modes other than SAS, the individual database management system (DBMS) tables are queried for the Available Tables and Available Columns lists. For DB2, DB2/2, DB2/6000, Sybase, and ODBC, the system tables information that fills the Available Tables and Available Columns can now be stored in SAS data sets. One data set contains Tables information. The other data set contains Columns information. When you use a remote session for querying, these SAS data sets can be stored locally for enhanced performance.

If you have read authority to the system tables, then you can assign the DB2, DB2/2, or DB2/6000 system tables to be read to SAS tables that are mirror images of the DB2 tables. If you are executing a remote session, then you can specify whether these SAS DB2 system tables are to be read locally or remotely.

You can create these mirror image tables by querying the DB2 system tables in an SQL Query Window session and creating SAS tables of the queries built. They can also be created with a PROC SQL program that queries the DB2 system tables. The PROC SQL statements can be saved and the SAS program can be run in batch whenever you need to update the mirror image tables.

SAS tables (data sets) that are created by automatic joins can also be created for any of the access modes that provide system tables/dictionaries with a PROC SQL program.

For ODBC, you can generate SAS data sets that contain system tables:

1 Select **Profile ▸ Set Preferences**.
2 In the Preference Settings for Profile window, set Access Mode to **ODBC**. Enter the data source, user name, and password, and select [OK].
3 In the Preference Settings for Profile window, select the right arrow next to [Access Mode Options].
4 In the Preference Settings for ODBC Access Mode window, enter the SAS data set names for system tables information.
5 If SAS data sets have not been created, then select [Create Table] and [Create Column].

For Sybase, the system table information can be read from a SAS data set:

1 Select **Profile ▸ Set Preferences**.
2 In the Preference Settings for Profile window, set Access Mode to **SYBASE**.
3 In the Sybase Access Mode Options window, enter the parameters for the Sybase access mode.
4 Select [SAS Data Sets].
5 In the Available Tables and Columns for Sybase window, enter the SAS library name and SAS data set name for Sybase system tables. If the Sybase system tables do not already exist, then select [Create Table] and [Create Column].

Handling Embedded Blanks in Column Names

DB2, DB2/2, DB2/6000, ORACLE, and ODBC column names can contain blanks. The SQL Query Window encloses column names in double quotation marks for these access modes to support any blanks within the column name string. Some ODBC drivers might not support double-quoted column names. To avoid conflicts with ODBC drivers, follow these steps:

1 Select **Profile ▶ Set Preferences**.

2 In the Preference Settings for Profile window, set Access Mode to **`ODBC`**. Enter the data source, user name, and password, and select [OK].

3 In the Preference Settings for ODBC Access Mode window, select **`Exclude double quote around column names`**.

Including Saved Queries

When you save a query, references in the query to tables are saved as two-level names (*libref.filename*). If you try to include a saved query that specifies a libref that is not currently assigned, or tables that have been moved or deleted, then the SQL Query Window will inform you that the tables cannot be found.

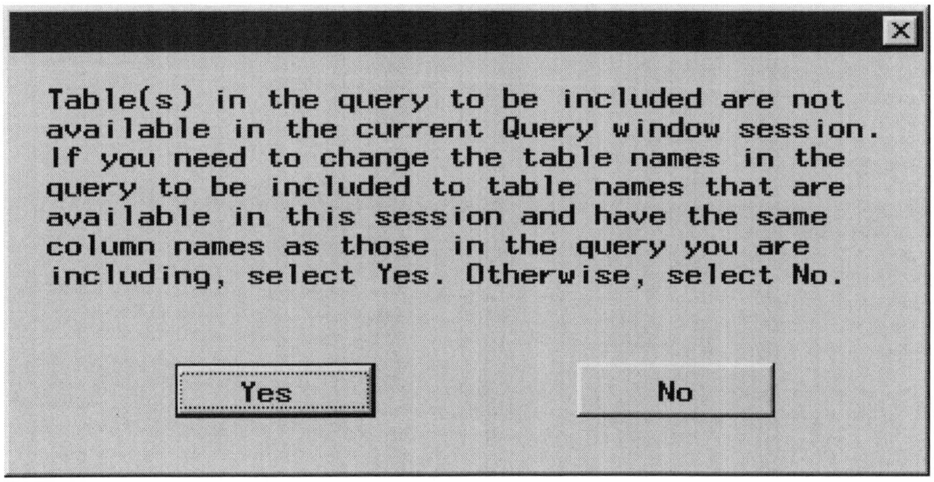

If the tables are available in another library, or if you want to run the query against different tables, then select [Yes]. The Include Query Tablename Edit window appears (probably with different names than in this example).

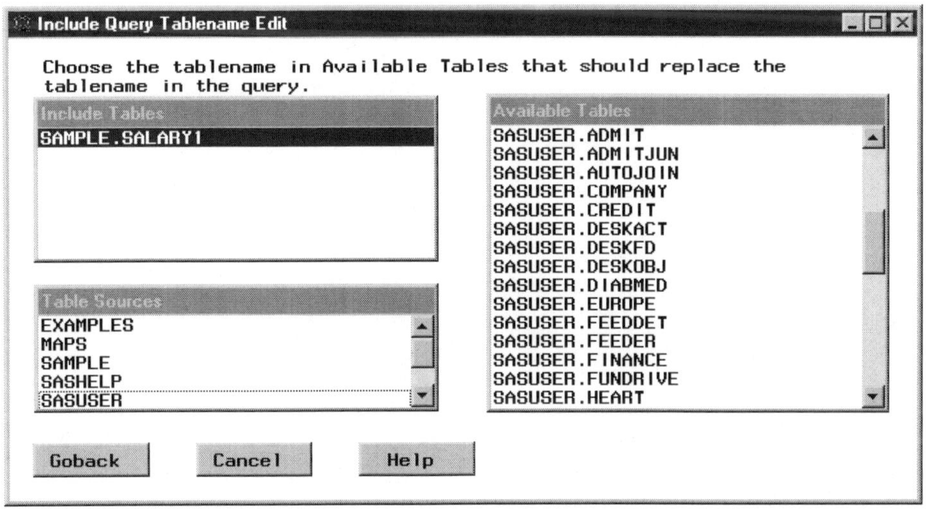

If the tables exist in another library, then select that library from the Table Sources list, and then select the tables from the Available Tables list.

If you want to run the query against different tables, then select the library that contains the tables from the Table Sources list, then select the tables from the Available Tables list. The tables must have identical structures to the tables on which the query was built.

This feature enables you to create a query that can be used on any identically structured table. For example, you could create a query on a table containing March sales data, and then use that query on a table containing April sales data. Remember that, to be prompted for a new table for the query, the original table on which the query was created must not be available in the SQL Query Window session. By moving the March table from, for example, the CUR_MON (Current Month) library, and moving the April table into the CUR_MON library, you would be prompted to supply the table for the query.

See "Saving Queries" on page 32 for more information about creating and saving queries.

APPENDIX
1

Recommended Reading

Recommended Reading

Here is the recommended reading list for this title:

- *Base SAS Procedures Guide*
- *Cody's Data Cleaning Techniques Using SAS Software*
- *Combining and Modifying SAS Data Sets: Examples*
- *SAS Language Reference: Concepts*
- *SAS Language Reference: Dictionary*
- *SAS SQL Procedure User's Guide*

For a complete list of SAS publications, see the current *SAS Publishing Catalog*. To order the most current publications or to receive a free copy of the catalog, contact a SAS representative at

SAS Publishing Sales
SAS Campus Drive
Cary, NC 27513
Telephone: (800) 727-3228*
Fax: (919) 677-8166
E-mail: **sasbook@sas.com**
Web address: **support.sas.com/publishing**
* For other SAS Institute business, call (919) 677-8000.

Customers outside the United States should contact their local SAS office.

Glossary

arithmetic operator
any of the symbols (+, -, /, *, and **) that are used to perform addition, subtraction, division, multiplication, or exponentiation in SAS expressions.

automatic join
a feature of the SQL Query Window that enables you to predefine join criteria for a specific set of tables. When you select these tables for a query in a future session, the join criteria are already defined and are ready for use.

automatic lookup
a feature of the SQL Query Window that automatically displays the values of a particular column when that column is selected in the WHERE EXPRESSION window.

automatic lookup table
a SAS data set that stores information that the SQL Query Window uses to determine how to perform automatic lookup. See also automatic lookup.

calculated column
in a query, a column that does not exist in any of the tables that are being queried, but which is created as a result of a column expression. See also column expression.

catalog
See SAS catalog.

column
in relational databases, a vertical component of a table. Each column has a unique name, contains data of a specific type, and has certain attributes. A column is analogous to a variable in SAS terminology.

column alias
a temporary, alternate name for a column. Aliases are optionally specified in the SQL procedure's SELECT clause to name or rename columns. An alias is one word. See also column.

column expression
a set of operators and operands that, when evaluated, result in a single data value. The resulting data value can be either a character value or a numeric value.

descriptive statistic
a quantity that characterizes, rather than draws inference from, a collection of values. Types of descriptive statistics are measures of central tendency, measures of variation among values, and measures of the shape of the distribution of values.

format
a pattern or set of instructions that SAS uses to determine how the values of a variable (or column) should be written or displayed. SAS provides a set of standard formats and also enables you to define your own formats.

group
in the SQL procedure, a set of rows that all have the same combination of values for the columns that are specified in a GROUP BY clause.

informat
a pattern or set of instructions that SAS uses to determine how data values in an input file should be interpreted. SAS provides a set of standard informats and also enables you to define your own informats.

inner join
See join.

join
in the SQL procedure, the combination of data from two or more tables (or from two or more SAS data views) to produce a single result table. A conventional join, which is often called an inner join, returns a result table for all the rows in one table that have one or more matching rows in the other table or tables. See also outer join.

join criteria
the set of parameters that determine how tables are to be joined. Join criteria are usually specified in a WHERE expression or in an SQL ON clause. See also join and outer join.

library engine
an engine that accesses groups of files and puts them in the correct form for processing by SAS utility windows and procedures. A library engine also determines the fundamental processing characteristics of the library and presents lists of files for the library directory.

libref (library reference)
a name that is temporarily associated with a SAS library. The complete name of a SAS file consists of two words, separated by a period. The libref, which is the first word, indicates the library. The second word is the name of the specific SAS file. For example, in VLIB.NEWBDAY, the libref VLIB tells SAS which library contains the file NEWBDAY. You assign a libref with a LIBNAME statement or with an operating system command.

logical operator
an operator that is used in expressions to link sequences of comparisons. The logical operators are AND, OR, and NOT.

missing value
in SAS, a term that describes the contents of a variable that contains no data for a particular row (or observation). By default, SAS prints or displays a missing numeric value as a single period, and it prints or displays a missing character value as a blank space. In the SQL procedure, a missing value is equivalent to an SQL NULL value.

null value
a special value that indicates the absence of information. Null values are analogous to SAS missing values.

operand
any of the variables and constants in a SAS expression that contain operators, variables, and constants.

operator
in a SAS expression, any of several symbols that request a comparison, a logical operation, or an arithmetic calculation.

outer join
in the SQL procedure, an inner join that is augmented with rows that do not match any row from the other table or tables in the join. There are three kinds of outer joins: left, right, and full. See also join.

profile
a set of parameters that control the behavior of the SQL Query Window.

query
a set of instructions that requests particular information from one or more data sources.

row
in relational database management systems, the horizontal component of a table. A row is analogous to a SAS observation.

SAS catalog
a SAS file that stores many different kinds of information in smaller units called catalog entries. A single SAS catalog can contain several different types of catalog entries. See also SAS catalog entry.

SAS catalog entry
a separate storage unit within a SAS catalog. Each entry has an entry type that identifies its purpose to SAS. Some catalog entries contain system information such as key definitions. Other catalog entries contain application information such as window definitions, Help windows, SAS formats and informats, macros, or graphics output.

SAS data set
a file whose contents are in one of the native SAS file formats. There are two types of SAS data sets: SAS data files and SAS data views. SAS data files contain data values in addition to descriptor information that is associated with the data. SAS data views contain only the descriptor information plus other information that is required for retrieving data values from other SAS data sets or from files that are stored in other software vendors' file formats.

SAS data view
a type of SAS data set that retrieves data values from other files. A SAS data view contains only descriptor information such as the data types and lengths of the variables (columns) plus other information that is required for retrieving data values from other SAS data sets or from files that are stored in other software vendors' file formats. SAS data views can be created by the SAS DATA step and by the SAS SQL procedure.

SQL (Structured Query Language)
a standardized, high-level query language that is used in relational database management systems to create and manipulate objects in a database management system. SAS implements SQL through the SQL procedure.

summary function
a function that summarizes or describes a group of data values, which are usually numeric data values. For example, SUM and MEAN are summary functions. See also descriptive statistic.

summary report
a report that provides a concise overview of information that is derived from one or more data sources. Summary information is typically calculated using descriptive statistics such as SUM, MEAN, and RANGE. See also descriptive statistic.

table
a two-dimensional representation of data in which the data values are arranged in rows and columns.

table source
a collection of one or more data sources to be queried.

view
a generic term (used by many software vendors) for a definition of a virtual data set (or table). The definition is named and stored for later use. A view contains no data; it merely describes or defines data that is stored elsewhere.

WHERE expression
a type of SAS expression that specifies a condition for selecting observations for processing by a DATA step or a PROC step. WHERE expressions can contain special operators that are not available in other SAS expressions. WHERE expressions can appear in a WHERE statement, a WHERE= data set option, a WHERE clause, or a WHERE command.

Index

O

P

Q

R

S

T

U

V

W

Your Turn

We welcome your feedback.

- If you have comments about this book, please send them to **yourturn@sas.com**. Include the full title and page numbers (if applicable).
- If you have comments about the software, please send them to **suggest@sas.com**.

1461007R0

Printed in Great Britain by
Amazon.co.uk, Ltd.,
Marston Gate.